"These are great practices—wise and straightforward, scientific and nourishing. They can transform your life."

> —Jack Kornfield, PhD, author of *The Wise Heart* and
> *A Path with Heart*

"Most people want to be happier, healthier, less stressed, and more self-accepting, but it's often hard to find time to work toward these goals. The brilliance of this book is that it offers powerful, targeted practices that can be done easily throughout the day to help people reach their highest potential."

> —Kristin Neff, PhD, associate professor at the University of
> Texas at Austin and author of *Self-Compassion*

"Delightfully clear and practical, this book distills profound insights from ancient wisdom traditions, modern psychology, and cutting-edge neurobiology into simple techniques anyone can use to live a happier, saner, more rewarding life. I felt more awake and alive after reading just a few pages."

> —Ronald D. Siegel, PsyD, assistant clinical professor
> of psychology at Harvard Medical School and author
> of *The Mindfulness Solution*

"If you are looking for bite-sized daily practices that can open your heart and clear your mind, *Just One Thing* deserves to be at the top of your reading list. Grounded in fascinating science, psychological understanding, and timeless wisdom, this book offers a rich assortment of entirely simple, doable ways you can find more happiness and ease."

> —Tara Brach, PhD, author of *Radical Happiness*

D0012614

"Rick Hanson has done the work for us, distilling decades of self-inquiry and key psychological research into fifty-two essential skills for healthy, happy living. This deceptively simple book is a trustworthy guide to living our lives more deeply and fully. Read, practice, and your brain will surely return the favor."

> —Christopher K. Germer, PhD, clinical instructor at
> Harvard Medical School and author of *The Mindful
> Path to Self-Compassion*

"This gem of a book is the perfect follow-up to Rick Hanson's brilliant *Buddha's Brain. Just One Thing* offers dozens of easy-to-learn practices that slowly work their magic on our brains, making it possible for all of us to dwell in the peaceful contentment of a Buddha. *Just One Thing* is one of those rare books that becomes a lifelong companion—never far out of reach."

> —Toni Bernhard, author of *How to Be Sick:
> A Buddhist-Inspired Guide for the Chronically Ill
> and their Caregivers*

"Is it improper to be begged by someone you don't know to buy a book? Then call me improper because I am begging you to give yourself the miracle of Rick Hanson's grounded science and earthy spirituality. Keep this book close by while giving copies to everyone you love."

> —Jennifer Louden, author of *The Woman's Comfort
> Book* and *The Life Organizer*

"What a way to go through life! These simple yet profound practices train the brain, open the heart, and enhance well-being. Rick Hanson provides the map. If you follow it, you'll surely increase your happiness and awaken your joy!"

> —James Baraz, author of *Awakening Joy*

"An owner's manual for the brain written in the simple, intuitive language our brains understand: short, pithy, easily-digestible nuggets that you can feel and remember. Extrapolating from neuroscience and skillfully synchronizing it with the insights of psychology and dharma, Hanson's voice shines through every page. Sane, helpful, deeply reassuring, and yet strong, clear, and penetrating, this is a helpful guide you can trust."

—Terry Patten, author of *Integral Life Practice*

"Just One Thing is just the thing for people who have full lives and can sometimes find only brief interludes for reflection and self-improvement. But don't be fooled—these bite-size chapters hold scientific insight, practical tools, and simple, direct, profound wisdom that will nourish your brain and your being as you navigate through daily life."

—Cassandra Vieten, PhD, director of research at the Institute of Noetic Sciences and author of *Living Deeply* and *Mindful Motherhood*

"Just One Thing is a brilliant, concise, and wise book for people who want to live with greater ease, joy, and skill. It clarifies the five foundations of living a great life and provides powerful practices to help people live more fully. While the form in which *Just One Thing* is written may appear simple, the messages are deep, profound, and useful. I highly recommend this book to anyone who dreams of thriving."

—Daniel Ellenberg, PhD, president of Relationships That Work

"Rick Hanson speaks from experience. He offers us simple, accessible, and fun insights and exercises that have real psychological benefits and practical value for a better life."

—Elisha Goldstein, PhD, author of *The Now Effect* and coauthor of *A Mindfulness-Based Stress Reduction Workbook*

"Anyone who thinks neuroscience is for the erudite will be pleasantly surprised by Rick Hanson's new book. *Just One Thing* has many, many things in store for readers, especially those interested in maximizing their brain potential, and, in fact, their life potential. Hanson not only presents a vast array of tried-and-true insights, but also spells out how each principle can be applied day by day and backs everything up with scientific understanding."

> —Stan Tatkin, PsyD, assistant clinical professor in the department of family medicine at the University of California, Los Angeles, and author of *Wired for Love*

"*Just One Thing* is just about everything you could want from a self-help book! It offers fascinating bits of information from recent neuroscience about our brains and nervous systems, along with simple exercises that can help us overcome our inherited programming. *Just One Thing* is a singular gift to us all!"

> —Wes Nisker, Buddhist meditation teacher, author, and performer

"The word that comes to mind when reading this gently wise book is kindness. Rick Hanson has a kindness that pervades the pages, while his writing remains grounded in science and spirituality. Peace and subtle change can arrive for you as you read and put into practice the compassionate, simple, yet powerful ideas and practices contained in *Just One Thing*."

> —Bill O'Hanlon, featured Oprah guest and author of *Do One Thing Different*

"All of these tiny prescriptions, each one wrapped around a nugget of wisdom, make a happy life seem feasible and within easy reach."

> —Sylvia Boorstein, PhD, author of *Happiness Is an Inside Job*

"Rick Hanson brings his compelling perspective—he is both a neuropsychologist and an experienced meditation practitioner—to this pragmatic consideration of wisdom practices. Down-to-earth and inspiring, *Just One Thing* is a companionable guidebook for inner travelers on a path of transformation, written by one who knows the territory well."

—Sharon Salzberg, author of *Real Happiness* and *Lovingkindness*

"By giving us simple practices for rewiring our neural networks, Rick Hanson is literally reminding us about what is truly important. I plan to devote a week to each of the fifty-two practices, taking this next year to cultivate the compassion at the heart of this book."

—Gordon Peerman, author of *Blessed Relief: What Christians Can Learn from Buddhists about Suffering*

"*Just One Thing* is more than just one more thing for you to read. It is Rick Hanson's gift drawn from four decades of learning about how to live with wisdom and peace. This book is filled with small, easy–to-understand lessons on how to live a meaningful life. These insights will surely enHanson your life! Each small essay explores the essential questions of our times: How do we find inner clarity in the face of outer turmoil? How do we feel less stress and learn to be more at home in our own skin? This gem of a book is filled with treasures that will build your relationships with others—and with yourself! I loved soaking in the clarity and sincerity of these offerings that invite us to enter life with more vitality and to live each day to the fullest. Feast on these pages and enjoy!"

—Daniel J. Siegel, MD, clinical professor at the University of California, Los Angeles School of Medicine and author of *Mindsight* and the *Pocket Guide to Interpersonal Neurobiology*

"There is joy and energy in learning to be kind to yourself and others. This book gently challenges you to do just that—step by step, practice by practice, day by day. The sense of wholeness that results will make a profound difference in your life."

—Steven C. Hayes, PhD, author of *Get Out of Your Mind and Into Your Life*

just
one
thing

developing a
buddha brain one simple
practice at a time

rick hanson, phd

new harbinger publications, inc.

Distributed in Canada by Raincoast Books

Copyright © 2011 by Rick Hanson
New Harbinger Publications, Inc.
5674 Shattuck Avenue
Oakland, CA 94609
www.newharbinger.com

Author photograph by Stephanie Mohan; Cover design by Amy Shoup; Text design by Michele Waters-Kermes; Acquired by Melissa Kirk

---

Library of Congress Cataloging-in-Publication Data

Hanson, Rick.
  Just one thing : developing a Buddha brain one simple practice at a time /
Rick Hanson.
    p. cm.
  Includes bibliographical references and index.
  ISBN 978-1-60882-031-3 (pbk.) -- ISBN 978-1-60882-032-0 (pdf e-book) 1.
Meditation--Buddhism. 2. Buddhism and science. 3. Happiness. 4. Wisdom.
I. Title.
  BQ5612.H36 2011
  294.3'444--dc23
                          2011020403

15   14

15   14   13   12   11   10   9   8   7

For Jan—my amazing, spectacular, and precious wife

Contents

part two:
Enjoy Life

part three:
Build Strengths

part four:
Engage the World

part five:
Be at Peace

introduction
Using Your Mind to
Change Your Brain

This is a book of practices—simple things you can do routinely, mainly inside your mind, that will support and increase your sense of security and worth, resilience, effectiveness, well-being, insight, and inner peace. For example, they include *taking in the good, protecting your brain, feeling safer, relaxing anxiety about imperfection, not knowing, enjoying your hands, taking refuge,* and *filling the hole in your heart.*

At first glance, you may be tempted to underestimate the power of these seemingly simple practices. But they will gradually change your brain through what's called *experience-dependent neuroplasticity.*

Moment to moment, whatever you're aware of—sounds, sensations, thoughts, or your most heartfelt longings—is based on underlying neural activities; the same goes for unconscious mental processes such as the consolidation of memory or the control of breathing. Exactly *how* the physical brain produces nonphysical consciousness remains a great mystery. But apart from the possible influence of transcendental factors—call them God, Spirit, the Ground, or by no name at all—there is a one-to-one mapping between mental and neural activities.

It's a two-way street: as your brain changes, your mind changes; and as your mind changes, your brain changes. This means—remarkably—that what you pay attention to, what you think and feel and want, and how you work with your reactions to things all sculpt your brain in multiple ways:

- Busy regions get more blood flow, since they need more oxygen and glucose.

- The genes inside neurons get more or less active; for example, people who routinely relax have improved expression of genes that calm down stress reactions, making them more resilient (Dusek et al. 2008).

- Neural connections that are relatively inactive wither away; it's a kind of neural Darwinism, the survival of the busiest: use it or lose it.

- "Neurons that fire together, wire together." This saying from the work of the psychologist Donald Hebb means that active synapses—the connections between neurons—get more sensitive, plus new synapses grow, producing thicker neural layers. For example, cab drivers who have to memorize the spaghetti snarl of streets in London have a thicker *hippocampus*—a part of the brain that helps make visual-spatial memories—at the end of their training (Maguire et al. 2000). Similarly, people who routinely practice mindfulness meditation develop thicker layers of neurons in the *insula*—a region that activates when you tune in to your body and your feelings—and in parts of the *prefrontal cortex* (in the front of your brain) that control attention (Lazar et al. 2005).

The details are complex, but the key point is simple: *how you use your mind changes your brain*—for better or worse.

There's a traditional saying that the mind takes the shape it rests upon; the modern update is that the *brain* takes the shape the mind rests upon. For instance, you regularly rest your mind upon worries, self-criticism, and anger, then your brain will gradually take the shape—will develop neural structures and dynamics—of anxiety, low sense of worth, and prickly reactivity to others. On the other hand, if you regularly rest your mind upon, for example, *noticing you're all right right now, seeing the good in yourself,* and *letting go*—three of the practices in this book—then your brain will gradually take the shape of calm strength, self-confidence, and inner peace.

You can't stop your brain from changing. The only question is: Are you getting the changes you want?

All It Takes Is Practice

That's where practice comes in, which simply means taking regular action—in thought, word, or deed—to increase positive qualities in yourself and decrease negative ones. For example, studies have shown that *being mindful* (chapter 22) increases activation of the left prefrontal cortex and thus lifts mood (since that part of the brain puts the brakes on negative emotions) (Davidson 2004), and it decreases activation of the *amygdala*, the alarm bell of the brain (Stein, Ives-Deliperi, and Thomas 2008). Similarly, *having compassion for yourself* (chapter 3) builds up resilience and lowers negative rumination (Leary et al. 2007; Neff 2009).

Basically, practice pulls weeds and plants flowers in the garden of your mind—and thus in your brain. That improves your garden, plus it makes you a better gardener: you get more skillful at directing your attention, thinking clearly, managing your feelings, motivating yourself, getting more resilient, and riding life's roller-coaster.

Practice also has built-in benefits that go beyond the value of the particular practice you're doing. For example, doing *any* practice is an act of kindness toward yourself; you're treating yourself like you matter—which is especially important and healing if you have felt as a child or an adult that others haven't respected or cared about you. Further, you're being active rather than passive—which increases optimism, resilience, and happiness, and reduces the risk of depression. At a time when people often feel pushed by external forces—such as financial pressures, the actions of others, or world events—and by their reactions to these, it's great to have at least some part of your life where you feel like a hammer instead of a nail.

Ultimately, practice is a process of personal transformation, gradually pulling the roots of greed, hatred, heartache, and delusion—broadly defined—and replacing them with contentment, peace, love, and clarity. Sometimes this feels like you're making changes inside yourself, and at other times it feels like you're simply uncovering wonderful, beautiful things that were always already there, like your natural wakefulness, goodness, and loving heart.

Either way, you're in the process of developing what one could call a "buddha brain," a brain that understands, profoundly, the causes of suffering and its end—for the root meaning of the word "buddha," is "to know, to awake." (I'm not capitalizing that word here in order to distinguish my general focus from the specific individual, the great teacher called the Buddha.) In this broad sense, anyone engaged in psychological growth or spiritual practice—whether Christian, Jewish, Muslim, Hindu, agnostic, atheist, or none of these—is developing a buddha brain and its related qualities of compassion, virtue, mindfulness, and wisdom.

The Law of Little Things

Now, if a practice is a hassle, most people (including me) are not going to do it. So the practices in this book involve either brief actions a few times a day—like *finding beauty* (chapter 17)—or simply a general attitude or perspective, such as *relaxing anxiety about imperfection* (chapter 46) or *not taking life so personally* (chapter 48).

Each moment of practice is usually small in itself, but those moments really add up. It's the law of little things: because of slowly accumulating changes in neural structure due to mental activity, lots of little things can wear down your well-being—and lots of little things can get you to a better place. It's like exercise: any single time you run, do Pilates, or lift weights won't make much difference—but over time, you'll build up your muscles. In the same way, small efforts made routinely will gradually build up the "muscle" of your brain. You really can have confidence, grounded in the latest brain science, that practice will pay off.

How to Use This Book

But you have to stick with it—so it really helps to focus on one main practice at a time. Life these days is so busy and complicated that it's great to have *just one thing* to keep in mind.

Of course, it's got to be the right "one thing." For forty years, I've been doing practices—first as a young person looking for happiness, then as a husband and father dealing with work and family life, and now as a neuropsychologist and meditation teacher—and teaching them to others. For this book, I've picked the best practices I know to build up the neural substrates—the foundations—of resilience, resourcefulness, well-being, and inner peace. I didn't invent a single one: they're the fundamentals that people make New Year's resolutions about but rarely do—and it's the *doing* that makes all the difference in the world.

You can do these practices in several ways. First, you could find one particular practice that by itself makes a big difference for you. Second, you can focus on the practices within a section of the book that addresses specific needs, such as part 1 on being good to yourself if you're self-critical, or part 5 on being at peace if you're anxious or irritable. Third, you could move around from practice to practice depending on what strikes your fancy or feels like it would help you the most right now. Fourth, you could take a week for each one of the fifty-two practices here, giving yourself a transformational "year of practice."

Whatever your approach is, I suggest you keep it simple and focus on one practice at a time—whether that time is an event or situation (e.g., a ticklish conversation with your mate, a crunch project at work, a meditation), a day, or longer. And in the back of your mind, other practices and their benefits can certainly be operating; for example, *not taking things personally* (chapter 48) could be in the foreground of awareness while *taking refuge* (chapter 28) is in the background.

Know what your practice is each day; the more you keep it in awareness, the more it will benefit you. Besides simply thinking about this practice from time to time, you could rest your mind even more upon it by putting up little reminders about it—such as a key word on a sticky note— or journaling about it or telling a friend what you're doing. You could also weave your practice into psychological or spiritual activities, such as psychotherapy, yoga, meditation, or prayer.

Working with just fifty-two practices, I've had to make some choices:

-   The practices are super-succinct; more could be said about each one of them. The title of each chapter is the practice. Chapters begin by answering *why* to do that practice, and then tell you *how* to do it. Chapter lengths vary depending on their subject.

-   With the exception of the very last practice, I've emphasized things done within yourself—such as *being grateful* (chapter 18)—rather than between yourself and others. (If you're interested in interpersonally focused practices in the *Just One Thing* (*JOT*) style, you might like my free e-newsletter by that name at www .RickHanson.net.) Meanwhile, you could apply the practices in this book to one or more relationships, or engage in them with a buddy—such as a friend or a mate—or as a group (e.g., family, team at work, reading group).

-   Most practices here involve taking action inside your mind—and of course it's also important to take action in your body and in the world around you.

-   There are three fundamental phases to psychological and spiritual growth: *being with* difficult material (e.g., old wounds, anger); *releasing* it; and *replacing* it with something more beneficial. In a nutshell, you let be, let go, and let in. You'll find practices for each of these phases, though I've concentrated on the third one because it's often the most direct and rapid way to reduce stress and unhappiness and develop positive qualities in yourself.

❧ While I experience and believe that something transcendental is involved with both mind and matter, I've stayed here within the frame of Western science.

As you engage these practices, have some fun with them. Don't take them (or yourself) too seriously. Feel free to be creative and adapt them to your own needs. For example, the *How* sections usually contain multiple suggestions, and you don't have to do all of them; just find the ones that do the most for you.

Throughout, take good care of yourself. Sometimes a practice will be too hard to sustain, or it will stir up painful issues. Then just drop it—for a while, or indefinitely. Draw on resources for practices; for example, deepening your sense of being cared about by others will help you *forgive yourself* (chapter 7). Remember that practice does not replace appropriate professional mental or physical health care.

Keep Going

People recognize that they've got to make an effort over time to become more skillful at driving a truck, running a department, or playing tennis. Yet it's common to think that becoming more skillful with one's own mind should somehow come naturally, without effort or learning.

But because the mind is grounded in biology, in the physical realm, the same laws apply: the more you put in, the more you get back. To reap the rewards of practice, you need to *do* it, and keep doing it.

Again, it's like exercise: if you do it only occasionally, you'll get only a little improvement; on the other hand, if you do it routinely, you'll get a large improvement. I've heard people talk like making efforts inside the mind is some kind of lightweight activity, but in fact it's always a matter of resolve and diligence—and sometimes it's very challenging and uncomfortable. Practice is not for wusses. You will *earn* its benefits.

So honor yourself for your practice. While it's down-to-earth and ordinary, it's also aspirational and profound. When you practice, you are nourishing, joining with, and uncovering the very best things about you. You are taking the high road, not the low one. You're drawing on sincerity, determination, and grit. You're taming and purifying the unruly mind—and the jungle that is the brain, with its reptilian, mammalian, and primate layers. You're offering beautiful gifts to your future self—the one being in the world you have the most power over and therefore the greatest duty to. And the fruits of your practice will ripple outward in widening circles, benefiting others, both known and unknown. Never doubt the power of practice, or how far your own chosen path of practice can take you.

I wish you the best on your path!

part one:

Be Good
to Yourself

1

Be for Yourself

To take any steps toward your own well-being—such as the practices in this book—you have got to be on your own side. Not against others, but *for* yourself.

For many people, that's harder than it sounds. Maybe you were raised to think you didn't count as much as other people. Maybe when you've tried to stick up for yourself, you've been blocked or knocked down. Maybe deep down you feel you don't deserve to be happy.

Think about what it's like to be a good friend to someone. Then ask: Am I that kind of friend to *myself*?

If not, you could be too hard on yourself, too quick to feel you're falling short, too dismissive of what you get done each day. Or too half-hearted about protecting yourself from mistreatment or telling others what you really need. Or too resigned to you own pain, or too slow about doing those things—both inside your head and outside it, in the wider world—to make your life better.

Plus, how can you truly help others if you don't start by helping yourself?

The foundation of all practice is to wish yourself well, to let your own sorrows and needs and dreams *matter* to you. Then, whatever you do for yourself will have real oomph behind it!

How

Several times a day, ask yourself: Am I on my own side here? Am I looking out for my own best interests? (Which will often include the best interests of others.)

Good times to do this:

- If you feel bad (e.g., sad, hurt, worried, disappointed, mistreated, frustrated, stressed, or irritated)

- If someone is pushing you to do something

- If you know you should do something for your own benefit but you're not doing it (like asserting yourself with someone, looking for a new job, or quitting smoking)

At these times, or in general:

- Bring to mind the feeling of being with someone who cares about you. This will help you feel like you matter and have worth, which is the basis of being for yourself.

❧ Recall what it feels like to be for someone. Perhaps a child, pet, or dear friend. Notice different aspects of this experience, such as loyalty, concern, warmth, determination, or advocacy. Let the sense of being on someone's side be big in your awareness. Let your body shift into a posture of support and advocacy: perhaps sitting or standing a little more erect, chest coming up a bit, eyes more intent; you're strengthening the experience of being for someone by drawing on embodied cognition, on the sensorimotor systems in your brain that underlie and shape your thoughts and feelings.

❧ Recall a time when you had to be strong, energetic, fierce, or intense on your own behalf. It could be as simple as the experience of the last part of an exercise routine, when you had to use every last ounce of willpower to finish it. Or it could be a time you had to escape from a serious danger, or stand up for yourself against an intimidating person, or doggedly grind out a big project in school or work. As in the bullet point just above, open to this experience and shift into embodying it so it is as real as possible for you, and so that you are stimulating and thus strengthening its underlying neural networks.

❧ See yourself as a young child—sweet, vulnerable, precious—and extend this same attitude of loyalty, strength, and caring toward that little boy or girl. (You could get a picture of yourself as a kid and carry it in your wallet or purse, and look at it from time to time.)

❧ Imagine having this same sense and stance of loyalty, strength, and caring for yourself today.

❧ Be mindful of what it feels like in your body to be on your own side. Open to and encourage that feeling as much as possible. Notice any resistance to it and try to let it go.

❧ Ask yourself: *Being on my own side, what's the best thing to do here?*

❧ Then, as best you can, do it.

Remember:

❧ Being for yourself simply means that you care about yourself. You wish to feel happy instead of worried, sad, guilty, or angry. You want people to treat you well instead of badly. You want to help your future self—the person you'll be next week, next year, next decade—to have as good a life as possible.

❧ Your experience *matters*, both for the moment-to-moment experience of living and for the lasting traces that your thoughts and feelings leave behind in the structure of your brain.

❧ It is moral to treat people with decency, respect, compassion, and kindness. Well, "people" includes you! You have as many rights, and your opinions and needs and dreams have as much standing, as those of anyone else in the world.

◄ When you take good care of yourself, then you have more to offer others, from the people close to you to the whole wide world.

2

Take in the Good

Scientists believe that your brain has a built-in *negativity bias* (Baumeister et al. 2001; Rozin and Royzman 2001). This is because, as our ancestors dodged sticks and chased carrots over millions of years of evolution, the sticks had the greater urgency and impact on survival.

This negativity bias shows up in lots of ways. For example, studies have found that:

- The brain generally reacts more to a negative stimulus than to an equally intense positive one (Baumeister et al. 2000).

- Animals—including us—typically learn faster from pain than from pleasure (Rozin and Royzman 2001); once burned, twice shy.

- Painful experiences are usually more memorable than pleasurable ones (Baumeister et al. 2001).

- Most people will work harder to avoid losing something they have than they'll work to gain the same thing (Rozin and Royzman 2001).

- Lasting, good relationships typically need at least a 5:1 ratio of positive to negative interactions (Gottman 1995).

In your own mind, what do you usually think about at the end of the day? The fifty things that went right, or the one that went wrong? Such as the driver who cut you off in traffic, or the one thing on your To Do list that didn't get done . . .

In effect, the brain is like Velcro for negative experiences, but Teflon for positive ones. That shades *implicit memory*—your underlying feelings, expectations, beliefs, inclinations, and mood—in an increasingly negative direction.

Which is not fair, since most of the facts in your life are probably positive or at least neutral. Besides the injustice of it, the growing pile of negative experiences in implicit memory naturally makes a person more anxious, irritable, and blue—plus it gets harder to be patient and giving toward others.

But you don't have to accept this bias! By tilting *toward* the good—toward that which brings more happiness and benefit to oneself and others—you merely level the playing field. Then, instead of positive experiences washing through you like water through a sieve, they'll collect in implicit memory deep down in your brain.

You'll still see the tough parts of life. In fact, you'll become more able to change them or bear them if you take in the good, since that will help put challenges in perspective, lift your energy and spirits, highlight useful resources, and fill up your own cup so you have more to offer to others.

And by the way, in addition to being good for adults, taking in the good is great for children, too, helping them to become more resilient, confident, and happy.

How

1. Look for good facts, and turn them into good experiences.

Good facts include positive events—like finishing a batch of e-mails or getting a compliment—and positive aspects of the world and yourself. Most good facts are ordinary and relatively minor—but they are still real. You are not looking at the world through rose-colored glasses, but simply recognizing something that is actual and true.

Then, when you're aware of a good fact—either something that currently exists or has happened in the past—let yourself *feel* good about it. So often in life a good thing happens—flowers are blooming, someone is nice, a goal's been attained—and you know it, but you don't feel it. This time, let the good fact affect you.

Try to do this step and the two that follow at least a half dozen times a day. When you do this, it usually takes only half a minute or so—there is always time to take in the good! You can do it on the fly in daily life, or at special times of reflection, like just before falling asleep (when the brain is especially receptive to new learning).

Be aware of any reluctance toward having positive experiences. Such as thinking that you don't deserve to, or that it's selfish, vain, or shameful to feel pleasure. Or that if you feel good, you will lower your guard and let bad things happen.

Then turn your attention back to the good facts. Keep opening up to them, breathing and relaxing, letting them move your needle. It's like sitting down to a meal: don't just look at it—taste it!

2. Really enjoy the experience.

Most of the time, a good experience is pretty mild, and that's fine. Simply stay with it for ten, twenty, even thirty seconds in a row—instead of getting distracted by something else.

Soften and open around the experience; let it fill your mind; give over to it in your body. (From a meditative perspective, this is a kind of concentration practice—for a dozen seconds or more—in which you become absorbed in a positive experience.) The longer that something is held in awareness and the more emotionally stimulating it is, the more neurons that fire and thus wire together, and the stronger the trace in implicit memory.

In this practice, you are not clinging to positive experiences, since that would lead to tension and disappointment. Actually, you are doing the opposite: by taking them in, you will feel better fed inside, and less fragile or needy. Your happiness will become more unconditional, increasingly based on an inner fullness rather than on external conditions.

3. Intend and sense that the good experience is sinking in to you.

People do this in different ways. Some feel it in the body as a warm glow spreading through the chest like the warmth of a cup of hot cocoa on a cold wintry day. Others visualize things like a golden syrup sinking down inside; a child might imagine a jewel going into a treasure chest in his or her heart. And some might simply know that while this good experience is held in awareness, its related neural networks are busily firing and wiring together.

Any single time of taking in the good will usually make just a little difference. But over time those little differences will add up, gradually weaving positive experiences into the fabric of your brain and your whole being.

In particular, as you do the practices in this book—or engage any process of psychological healing and growth, or spiritual development—really take in the fruits of your efforts. Help them stick to your mental/neural ribs!

3

Have Compassion for Yourself

Life is full of wonderful experiences. But it has its hard parts as well, such as physical and mental discomfort, ranging from subtle to agonizing. This is the realm of suffering, broadly defined.

When someone you care about suffers, you naturally have *compassion*: the wish that a being not suffer, usually with a feeling of sympathetic concern. For example, if your child falls and hurts himself, you want him to be out of pain; if you hear that a friend is in the hospital, or out of work, or going through a divorce, you feel for her and hope that everything will be all right. Compassion is in your nature: it's an important part of the neural and psychological systems we evolved to nurture children, bond with mates, and hold together "the village it takes to raise a child" (Goetz, Keltner, and Simon-Thomas 2010).

You can also have compassion for yourself—which is *not* self-pity. You're simply recognizing that "this is tough, this hurts," and bringing the same warmhearted wish for suffering to lessen or end that you would bring to any dear friend grappling with the same pain, upset, or challenge as you.

Studies have shown that self-compassion has many benefits (Leary et al. 2007; Neff 2009), including:

- Reducing self-criticism
- Lowering stress hormones like cortisol
- Increasing self-soothing, self-encouragement, and other aspects of resilience
- Helping to heal any shortages of caring from others in your childhood

That's a pretty good list!

Self-compassion usually takes only a handful of seconds. And then—more centered and heartened—you can get on with doing what you can to make your life better.

How

Maybe your back hurts, or you've had a miserable day at work, or someone has barked at you unfairly. Or, honestly, maybe you just feel bad, even depressed. Whatever it is, some self-compassion could help. Now what?

Self-compassion comes naturally for some people (particularly those with a well-nurtured childhood). But it's not that easy for a lot of us, especially those who are self-critical, driven, stoic, or think it's self-indulgent to be caring toward themselves.

So here are some steps for calling up self-compassion, which you could blend together as self-compassion becomes easier for you:

- Take a moment to acknowledge your difficulties: your challenges and suffering.

- Bring to mind the feeling of being with someone you *know* cares about you. Perhaps a dear friend, a family member, a spirit, God . . . even a pet. Let yourself feel that you matter to this being, who wants you to feel good and do well in life.

- Bring to mind your difficulties, and imagine that this being who cares about you is feeling and expressing compassion for you. Imagine his or her facial expression, gestures, stance, and attitude toward you. Let yourself receive this compassion, taking in its warmth, concern, and goodwill. Open to feeling more understood and nurtured, more peaceful and settled. The experience of *receiving* caring primes circuits in your brain to *give* it.

- Imagine someone you naturally feel compassion for: perhaps a child, or a family member. Imagine how you would feel toward that person if he or she were dealing with whatever is hard for you. Let feelings of compassion fill your mind and body. Extend them toward that person, perhaps visualized as a kind of light radiating from you (maybe from your heart). Notice what it's like to be compassionate.

※ Now, extend the same sense of compassion toward yourself. Perhaps accompany it with words like these, heard softly in the back of your mind: *May this pain pass . . . may things improve for me . . . may I feel less upset over time.* Have some warmth for yourself, some acknowledgment of your own difficulties and pain, some wish for things to get better. Feel that this compassion is sinking in to you, becoming a part of you, soothing and strengthening you.

4

Relax

It's easy to feel stressed these days. Or worried, frustrated, or irritated about one thing or another, such as finances, work, the health of a family member, or a relationship.

When you get stressed or upset, your body *tenses up* to fight, flee, or freeze. That's Mother Nature's way, and its short-term benefits kept our ancestors alive to pass on their genes.

But today—when people can live seventy or eighty years or more, and when quality of life (not mere survival) is a priority—we pay a high, long-term price for daily tension. It leads to health problems like heart disease, poor digestion, backaches and headaches, and hormonal ups and downs. And to psychological problems, including anxiety, irritability, and depression.

The number one way to reduce tension is through relaxation. Besides its benefits for physical and mental health, relaxation feels great. Just recall how nice it feels to soak in a tub, curl up in bed, or plop on the couch after the dishes are done.

Whether you're stuck in traffic, wading through an overflowing in-box, or having a tough conversation, being able to relax your body at will is a critically important inner skill.

How

Here are some good ways to activate the "rest-and-digest" *parasympathetic nervous system* (PNS) that calms down the fight-or-flight *sympathetic nervous system*:

- PNS fibers, involved with digestion, fill the mouth. So relax your tongue and jaw; perhaps touch your lips. (If I'm having a hard time sleeping, sometimes I'll rest a knuckle against my lips, which has a soothing and calming effect.)

- Open your lips slightly. This can help ease stressful thinking by reducing subvocalizations, the subtle, unconscious movements of the jaw and tongue often associated with mental speech.

- Do several long exhalations, since the PNS handles exhaling. For example inhale for a count of three, and exhale for a count of six.

- For a minute or more, breathe in such a way that your inhalation and exhalation are equally long; count mentally up to five for each inhalation and each exhalation. This creates small but smooth changes in the interval between heartbeats— since the heart speeds up slightly with inhalation and slows down slightly with exhalation—which is associated with relaxation and well-being (Kristal-Boneh et al. 1995).

- Relax your diaphragm—the muscle underneath your lungs that helps suck air into them—by putting your hand on your stomach, just below your rib cage, and then trying to breathe in a way that pushes your hand half an inch or so away from your backbone. (This is especially helpful if you're feeling anxious.)

- Try these methods in stressful situations, or any time you're feeling worried or frustrated; they really work! Also use them "offline," when things are more settled, such as by setting aside a few minutes each day—perhaps just before bed—to practice relaxation. The resting state of your body-mind will become more peaceful, and you'll become more resilient when things hit the fan. For example, researchers have found that practicing relaxation actually increases the expression of genes that calm down the stress response (Dusek et al. 2008).

5

See the Good in Yourself

There is good in every person—but it's often easier to see in others than in yourself. For example, think about a friend: What do you like about him or her? Including qualities such as sense of humor, fairness, honesty, intelligence, soul, patience, passion, helpfulness, curiosity, determination, talent, spunk, or a good heart.

Seeing these positive characteristics in your friend feels reassuring, comfortable, and hopeful. It's good to recognize what's good in someone.

Including you!

Each of us is like a mosaic, with lots of lovely tiles, some that are basically neutral, and a few that could use a little—ah—work. It's important to see the whole mosaic. But because of the brain's negativity bias, we tend to fixate on what's wrong with ourselves instead of what's right. If you do twenty things in a day and nineteen go fine, what's the one you think about? Probably the one that didn't go so well.

Your brain builds new structures primarily based on what you pay attention to; neurons that fire together, wire together. Focusing on the "bad" tiles in the mosaic you are reinforces an underlying sense of being mediocre, flawed, or less than others. And it blocks the development of the confidence and self-worth that come from recognizing the good tiles. These results of the negativity bias are not fair. But they're sure powerful, and a big reason most of us have feelings of inadequacy or self-doubt; I've had to work with these issues myself.

Knowing your own strengths and virtues is just a matter of seeing yourself *accurately.* Then, recognizing the good in yourself, you'll feel better inside, reach out to others with less fear of rejection, and pursue your dreams with more confidence that you'll have success.

How

Pick one simple good thing about yourself. Maybe you are particularly friendly, open, conscientious, imaginative, warm, perceptive, or steadfast. Be aware of the experience of that positive characteristic. Explore its body sensations, emotional tones, and any attitudes or viewpoints that go with it.

Take a little time to register that you do indeed have this good quality. Let yourself become convinced of it.

Look for signs of it for a day or a week—and feel it when you find it.

Notice any difficulty in accepting that you have this good quality, such as thoughts like *But I'm not that way all the time.* Or *But I have bad parts, too.* Try to get on your own side here and see yourself realistically, including your good qualities. It's okay that you don't live from those qualities every minute: that's what it means to be a mosaic; that's what it means to be human.

Repeat this process for other strengths or virtues that you have.

Also open to the good things that *others* recognize in you. Start with a friend, and look at yourself through his or her eyes. What does that person like about you? Or appreciate, enjoy, respect, or admire? If your friend were telling someone else about your good qualities, what might he or she say? Do this again with several other people from different parts—and perhaps times—of your life, such as other friends or a family member, partner, teacher, coach, or coworker. Then allow other people's knowing of your good characteristics to become your own. Soften your face and body and mind to take in this knowing of the truth, the whole truth, of your personal mosaic.

Whether it starts with your own recognition of yourself or from other people, let the knowing of good things about you become feelings of worth, confidence, happiness, and peace.

Sense a quiet voice inside you, coming from your own core, firmly and honestly listing some of your good qualities. Listen to it. Let what it's saying sink in. If you like, write down the list and go over it from time to time; you don't have to show it to anyone.

As you go through life, look for examples of your decency, endurance, caring, and other good qualities. When you see these facts, open to feeling good about yourself.

Let these times of feeling good about yourself gradually fill your heart and your days.

6

Slow Down

Most of us are running around way too much. Say you bump into a friend you haven't seen for a while and ask, "How are you?" Twenty years ago, a typical answer would be "fine." But today the reply is more likely to be "busy!"

We're caught up in e-mails, phone calls, long hours working, schlepping kids from here to there, and trying to match velocities with everyone else who has speeded up.

Whatever the particular causes may be in your own life, it's easy to feel like a short-order cook at the lunch rush.

There's a place for revving up occasionally, whether it's dealing with an emergency or cheering like a maniac because your fourth-grade daughter has finally taken a shot while playing basketball (that was me).

But chronic speediness has many bad effects:

- ❧ It activates the same general stress-response system that evolved in the brain to protect us from charging lions, which releases nerve-jangling hormones like adrenaline and cortisol, weakens your immune system, and wears down your mood.

- ❧ It puts the alarm system of the brain on red alert, scanning for threats and often overreacting. Have you ever noticed that when you speed up, you're quicker to find things to worry or get irritated about?

- ❧ It gives you less time to think clearly and make good decisions.

Even though "the need for speed" may have become a way of life, it's always possible to make a change. Start with little things. And then let them grow. Honestly, slowing down is one of those seemingly small actions that could really change your life.

How

Here are some ways to slow down. I suggest doing just a few of them: don't rush to slow down!

- ❧ Do a few things more slowly than usual. Leisurely lift the cup to your lips, don't rush through a meal, let others finish talking before jumping in, or stroll to a meeting instead of racing. Finish one task before moving on to another. A few times a day, take a long, *slow* breath.

⊷ Back off the gas pedal. One time, as I zoomed down the freeway, my wife murmured, "What's the rush?" She made me realize that slowing down a few miles per hour meant arriving just a few minutes later, but with lots more ease along the way.

⊷ When the phone rings, imagine that it is a church or temple bell reminding you to breathe and slow down. (This suggestion is from the Vietnamese monk Thich Nhat Hanh.)

⊷ Resist the pressure of others to get things done sooner than you really need to. As the saying has it, their lack of planning does not make it your emergency.

⊷ Find what's good about this moment as it is, so you'll have less need to zip along to the next thing. For example, if you're stuck on hold on a phone call, look around for something that's beautiful or interesting, or enjoy the peacefulness of simply breathing.

Over time, wrap up existing commitments and be careful about taking on new ones. Notice and challenge any internal pressure to always be doing and getting more and more. What's the net bottom-line effect on your quality of life: Does racing about make you happier? Or more stressed and worn out?

All the while, soak in the ease and well-being that come from slowing down—and don't be surprised if people say you look more confident, rested, dignified, and happy.

It's *your* life, no one else's. Slow down and enjoy it!

7

Forgive Yourself

Everyone messes up. Me, you, the neighbors, everybody. It's important to acknowledge mistakes, learn from them so they don't happen again, and feel appropriate remorse. But most people keep beating themselves up way past the point of usefulness: they're unfairly self-critical.

Inside the mind are many subpersonalities. For example, one part of me sets the alarm clock for 6 a.m. to get up and exercise . . . and then when it goes off, another part of me grumbles: *Who set the darn clock*?! More broadly, there are an inner critic and an inner protector inside each of us. For most people, that inner critic is continually yammering away, looking for something, anything, to find fault with. It magnifies small failings into big ones, punishes you over and over for things long past, ignores the larger context, and doesn't credit you for your efforts to make amends.

That's why you need your inner protector to stick up for you: to put your weaknesses and misdeeds in perspective, to highlight your many good qualities surrounding your lapses, to encourage you to return to the high road even if you've gone down the low one, and—frankly—to tell that inner critic to Hush Up Now.

How

Start by picking something relatively small that you're still being hard on yourself about, and try the methods below. Then work up to more significant issues.

Here we go:

- Start by getting in touch with the feeling of being cared about by someone in your life today or from your past. Get a sense that this person's caring for you, and perhaps other aspects of him or her, have been taken into your own mind as parts of your inner protector. Do this with other beings who care about you, and open to a growing sense of your inner protector.

- Staying with feeling cared about, bring to mind some of your many good qualities. You could ask the protector what it knows about you. These are facts, not flattery, and you don't need a halo to have good qualities like patience, determination, fairness, or kindness.

⁂ This step and the one above it will help you face whatever needs forgiving, and actually forgive yourself.

⁂ If you yelled at a child, lied at work, partied too hard, let a friend down, cheated on a partner, or were secretly glad about someone's downfall—*whatever* it was—acknowledge the facts: what happened, what was in your mind at the time, the relevant context and history, and the results for yourself and others.

⁂ Notice any facts that are hard to face—like the look in a child's eyes when you yelled at her—and be especially open to them; they're the ones that are keeping you stuck. It is always the truth that sets us free.

⁂ Sort what happened into three piles: moral faults, unskillfulness, and everything else. Moral faults deserve *proportionate* guilt, remorse, or shame, but unskillfulness calls for correction, no more. (This point is *very* important.)

You could ask others—including people you may have wronged—what they think about this sorting (and about other points below), but you alone get to decide what's right. For example, if you gossiped about someone and embellished a mistake he made, you might decide that the lie in your exaggeration is a moral fault deserving a wince of remorse, but that casual gossip (which most of us do at one time or another) is simply unskillful and should be corrected (i.e., not done again) without self-flagellation.

* In an honest way, take responsibility for your moral fault(s) and unskillfulness. Say in your mind or out loud (or write): *I am responsible for* _____ , _____ , *and* _____ . Let yourself *feel* it.

Then add to yourself: *But I am NOT responsible for* _____ , _____ , *and* _____ . For example, you are not responsible for the misinterpretations or overreactions of others. Let the relief of what you are NOT responsible for sink in.

* Acknowledge what you have already done to learn from this experience, and to repair things and make amends. Let this sink in. Appreciate yourself.

Next decide what, if anything, remains to be done—inside your own heart or out there in the world—and then do it. Let it sink in that you're doing it, and appreciate yourself for this, too.

Now check in with your inner protector: is there anything else you should face or do? Listen to the still, quiet voice of conscience, so different from the pounding scorn of the critic. If you truly know that something remains, then take care of it. But otherwise, know in your heart that what needed learning has been learned, and that what needed doing has been done.

- And now actively forgive yourself. Say in your mind, out loud, in writing, or perhaps to others statements like *I forgive myself for* _____ , _____ , *and* _____ . *I have taken responsibility and done what I could to make things better.* You could also ask the inner protector to forgive you, or others out in the world, such as the person you wronged.

- You may need to go through one or more of the steps above again and again to truly forgive yourself, and that's alright. Allow the experience of being forgiven—in this case, by yourself—to take some time to sink in. Help it sink in by opening up to it in your body and heart, and by reflecting on how it will help others if you stop beating yourself up.

May you be at peace.

8
Get More Sleep

You need more sleep.

That is, unless you really are that rare person these days who's truly getting enough sleep. (Disclosure: that person is definitely not me.)

Without sufficient sleep, risks go up for car accidents, diabetes, heart disease, depression, and unwanted weight. And performance goes down in paying attention, learning, and staying motivated. Plus, it just feels bad to be foggy, groggy, tired, and irritable.

People don't get enough sleep for a variety of reasons. It's common to stay up too late and get up too early, and drink too much coffee to get going in the morning and too much alcohol to relax at night. Sleep problems are also a symptom of some health conditions—such as depression and sleep apnea—so talk with your doctor if you have insomnia or if you still feel tired after seemingly getting enough sleep.

The right amount of sleep varies from person to person—and from time to time: if you're stressed, ill, or working hard, you need more sleep. Whatever it is that you need, the key is consistency: getting good rest every night, not trying to catch up on weekends or holidays.

After I left home, I often went back to visit my parents. They frequently told me I looked tired and needed more sleep. It bugged me every time they said it. But you know what?

They were right. Almost everyone needs more sleep.

How

Two things get in the way of sufficient sleep: not setting enough time aside for it, and not having deep and continuous sleep during the time allotted.

In terms of the first problem:

- Decide how much time you want to sleep each night. Then, look at your schedule, see when you need to wake up, and work backwards to give yourself a bedtime. Figure out what you need to do during the hour before your bedtime to get to sleep on time; it probably includes not getting into an argument with anyone!

- Observe the "reasons" that emerge to stay up past your bedtime. Most if not all of them will boil down to a basic choice: what's more important, your health and well-being—or watching another hour of TV, doing housework, or (fill in the blank)?

- Really enjoy feeling rested and alert when you get enough sleep. Take in those good feelings, so your brain will want more of them in the future.

In terms of the second problem, issues with sleep itself, here are some suggestions; pick the ones that work for you:

- Consider the advice of organizations like the National Sleep Foundation: have a bedtime routine; relax in the last hour or two before bed; stop eating (particularly chocolate), drinking coffee or alcohol, exercising, or smoking cigarettes two or three hours before bedtime; make sure the environment of your bedroom supports sleep (e.g., cool and quiet, good mattress, earplugs if your partner snuffles or snores).

- Do what you can to lower stress. Chronic stress raises hormones like cortisol, which will make it hard to fall asleep in the first place, or wake up early in the morning.

- Make a deal with yourself to worry or plan during the next day, after you get up. Shift your attention to things that make you feel happy and relaxed, or simply to the sensations of breathing itself. Bring to mind the warm feeling of being with people who care about you. Have compassion for yourself.

- Really relax. For example, take five to ten *long* exhalations; imagine your hands are warm (and tuck them under the pillow); rest a finger or knuckle against your lip; relax your tongue and jaw; imagine you are in a very peaceful setting; progressively relax each part of your body, starting with your feet and moving up to your head.

❧ Certain nutrients are important for sleep. Unless you're sure you're getting these in your daily diet, consider supplementing magnesium (500 milligrams/day) and calcium (1200 milligrams/day). If you can, take half in the morning and half before bed.

❧ The neurotransmitter serotonin aids sleep; it is made from an amino acid, tryptophan, so consider taking 500–1000 milligrams of tryptophan just before bed. If you wake up in the middle of the night and can't easily fall back to sleep, consider 1 milligram of melatonin taken sublingually (under the tongue). You could also eat a banana or something else that's quick and easy; rising blood sugar will lift insulin levels, which will help transport more tryptophan into your brain. You can usually get tryptophan and melatonin at a health food store; do not supplement either of these if you are breastfeeding or taking psychiatric medication (unless your doctor tells you it's fine).

Good night!

9

Befriend Your Body

Imagine that your body is separate from you, and consider these questions:

- How has your body taken care of you over the years? Such as keeping you alive, giving you pleasure, and taking you from place to place.

- In return, how well do you take care of your body? Such as soothing, feeding, and exercising it, or taking it to the doctor. On the other hand, in what ways might you run it down, feed it junk food, or intoxicate it?

- In what ways are you critical of your body? For example, are you disappointed in it or embarrassed by it? Do you feel let down by it, or wish it were different?

- If your body could talk to you, what might it say?

◦ If your body were a good friend, how would you treat it? Would that be different from how you treat it now?

Personally, I can't help squirming a little when I face these questions myself. It's common to push the body hard, ignore its needs until they get intense, and tune out from its signals. And then drop the body into bed at the end of another long day like—as my father would say, having grown up on a ranch—"a horse rid hard and put up wet."

People can also get mad at the body, and even mean to it. Like it's the body's fault if it weighs too much or is getting old.

But if you do any of these things, you'll end up paying a big price, since you are not separated from your body after all. Its needs and pleasures and pains are your own. Its fate will be your own someday.

On the other hand, if you treat your body well, like a good friend, you'll feel better, have more energy, be more resilient, and probably live longer.

How

Remember a time when you treated a good friend well. What was your attitude toward your friend, and what kinds of things did you do with him or her? How did it feel inside to be nice toward your friend?

Next, imagine a day of treating your body like another good friend. Imagine loving this friend—your body—as you wake up and help it out of bed: being gentle with it, staying connected to it, not rushing about . . . what would this feel like?

Imagine cherishing your body as you move through the morning—such as helping it kindly to some water, giving it a nice shower, and serving it healthy and delicious food. Imagine treating your body with love as you do other activities, such as driving, caring for children, exercising, working with others, doing dishes, having sex, or brushing your teeth.

How would this approach feel?

You'd probably experience less stress, more relaxation and calm, more pleasure, more ease, and more of a sense of being in control of your life. Plus an implicit sense of being kind to yourself, since in a deep sense you don't just have a body, you are your body; treating it well is treating *you* well.

If your body could speak, what might it say to you after being treated with love for a day?

Then, for real, treat your body well for a day (or even for just a few minutes). What's this like? In what ways does it feel good? Notice any reluctance to be nice to your body. Maybe a feeling that doing so would be self-indulgent or sinful. Explore that reluctance, and see what it's about. Then decide if it makes any sense. If it doesn't, return to treating your body well.

If you could talk to your body, what might you say? Perhaps write a letter to your body, telling it how you've felt about it in the past, and how you want to be nicer to it in the future.

Make a short list of how to care better for your body, such as quitting smoking, or leaving work sooner, or taking more time for simple bodily pleasures. Then commit to treating your body better.

Kindness begins at home.

Your home is your body.

10
Nourish Your Brain

Your brain contains about a hundred billion neurons plus another trillion support cells. Most neurons fire five to fifty times a second—even when you're asleep. Consequently, even though your brain weighs only three pounds, about 2 to 3 percent of bodyweight, it needs about 25 percent of the glucose in your blood. No wonder it's hungry!

And it needs other nutrients besides glucose. For example, about 60 percent of the dry weight of the brain consists of healthy fats. Or consider the neurotransmitters that carry information from one neuron to another. Your body builds these complex molecules from smaller parts, assisted by other biochemicals. For instance, serotonin—which supports your mood, digestion, and sleep—is made from tryptophan with the aid of iron and vitamin B_6.

Significant shortages in any one of the dozens of nutrients your brain needs will harm your body and mind. For example:

Shortage	Effect
Vitamins B_{12}, B_6, folate	Depressed mood (Skarupski, et al, 2010)
Vitamin D	Weaker immune system; dementia; depressed mood (Nimitphong and Holick 2011)
DHA	Depressed mood (Rondanelli et al. 2010)

On the other hand, filling up your neural cupboard with good supplies will bring you more energy, resilience, and well-being.

How

At every meal, especially breakfast, have three to four ounces of protein—about the size of a deck of cards—from one source or another. This will give you vital amino acids plus help regulate blood sugar and insulin.

Speaking of blood sugar, eating lots of sweets and white-flour carbohydrates raises insulin levels . . . which then crash, leading to the weary/cranky/foggy state of hypoglycemia. Routinely high insulin also puts you on the slippery slope to type 2 diabetes. So keep these foods to a minimum, aiming for no more than twenty-five grams a day of refined sugar, and avoiding refined flours as much as possible.

Eat lots of dark-colored fruits and vegetables, such as blueberries, kale, beets, carrots, and broccoli. These foods contain important nutrients that support memory (Krikorian, et al. 2010), protect your brain against oxidation (Guerrero-Beltran, et al. 2010), and may reduce the risk of dementia (Gu, et al. 2010).

Take a broad-spectrum, high-potency, multivitamin/ mineral supplement. It would be great if you could get all the nutrients for optimal health from three meals a day, but most people don't have the time to get and prepare all the fresh vegetables and other complex foods this would take. Plus we need more of these nutrients to help metabolize the hundreds of man-made molecules we're exposed to each day. In addition to eating as healthily as you can, it's simple to toss a few supplement capsules a day down the hatch, which takes less time than brushing your teeth. To identify a high-quality supplement—whose daily dose probably involves two to three capsules—look for one that has about five to ten times the "daily values" (DVs) of B vitamins and 100 percent of the DVs of minerals.

Also take two to three capsules a day of high-quality fish oil, enough to get at least 500 milligrams of both DHA (decosahexaenoic acid) and EPA (eicosapentaenoic acid); check the label. If you don't want fish oil, an alternative is a combination of flax oil and DHA from algae, but fish oil is the most effective way to get omega-3 oils into your body and brain.

Meanwhile, as you take these actions, enjoy knowing that as you "feed your head," you're in fact feeding your life.

11

Protect Your Brain

Your brain controls your other bodily systems, and it's the basis for your thoughts and feelings, joys and sorrows. No question, it is the most important organ in your body. Small changes in its neurochemistry can lead to big changes in your mood, resilience, memory, concentration, thoughts, feelings, and desires.

So it's vital to protect it from negative factors like toxins, inflammation, and stress.

If you take good care of your brain, it will take good care of you.

How

Avoid toxins. Besides the obvious actions—like don't sniff glue, and stand upwind when pumping gas—be careful about alcohol, which works by depriving brain cells of oxygen: that buzz is the feeling of neurons drowning.

Minimize inflammation. When your immune system activates to deal with an infection or allergen, it sends chemical messengers called *cytokines* throughout your body. Unfortunately, cytokines can linger in your brain, leading to a slump in mood and even depression (Maier and Watkins 1998; Schiepers, Wichers, and Maes 2005).

So take practical steps to reduce colds and flu, such as washing your hands often, and avoid any foods that set off your immune system. For example, many people have inflammatory reactions to gluten grains (e.g., wheat, oats, rye) and/or dairy products; it's not surprising, since these foods were introduced just 10,000 years ago, a tiny moment in the 200 million-year evolution of the mammalian, primate, and human diet. You don't need overt symptoms of allergies for a medical lab blood test to show that gluten or dairy foods aren't good for you. On your own, try going to zero with both these food groups for two weeks and see if you notice a difference in your mental or physical health; if you do, keep staying away from them: I do myself, and there are plenty of delicious alternatives.

Get regular exercise, which promotes the growth of new neural structures, including via the birth of new brain cells.

Relax. The stress hormone cortisol both sensitizes the fight-or-flight alarm bell of the brain—the amygdala—and weakens (even shrinks) a region called the hippocampus, which helps put the brakes on stress reactions. Consequently, in a vicious cycle, stress today makes you more sensitive to stress tomorrow. Additionally, since the hippocampus is also critical for making memories, a daily diet of stress (even from just feeling frustrated, irritated, or anxious) makes it harder to learn new things or put your feelings in context. One major antidote to stress is relaxation, which activates the soothing and calming parasympathetic wing of the nervous system; see chapter 4 for good ways to relax.

part two:

Enjoy Life

12
Take Pleasure

When you find pleasure in life, you are not pushing away things that are hard or painful. You are simply opening up to the sweet stuff that's already around you—and basking, luxuriating, and delighting in it.

This activates the calming and soothing parasympathetic wing of your autonomic nervous system, and quiets the fight-or-flight sympathetic wing and its stress-response hormones. Besides lifting your mood, settling your fears, and brightening your outlook, the stress relief of taking pleasure offers physical health benefits, too: strengthening your immune system, improving digestion, and balancing hormones.

How

Relish the pleasures of daily life, starting with your senses:

- *What smells good?* The skin of an orange, wood smoke on the air, dinner on the stove, a young child's hair . . .

- *Tastes delicious?* Strong coffee, delicate tea, French toast—chocolate!—tossed salad, goat cheese . . .

- *Looks beautiful?* Sunrise, sunset, full moon, a baby sleeping, red leaves in autumn, images of galaxies, fresh fallen snow . . .

- *Sounds wonderful?* Waves on the seashore, wind through pine trees, a dear friend laughing, Beethoven's Ode to Joy, silence itself . . .

- *Feels good on your skin?* Newly washed sheets, a good back scratch, warm water, a fresh breeze on a muggy day . . .

Next, include the mind: What do you like to think about or remember. For example, bring to mind a favorite setting—a mountain meadow, a tropical beach, a cozy living room chair—and imagine yourself there.

Last, *savor* these pleasures. Sink into them, take your time with them, and let them fill your body and mind. Marinate in pleasure! Notice any resistance to feeling really good, any thought that it is foolish or wrong . . . and then see if you can let that go. And fall back into pleasure.

Enjoy yourself!

13

Say Yes

When our son was doing theater in high school, I learned about an exercise for improvisational acting ("improv"): no matter what another actor says or does to you, you are always supposed to figuratively (and sometimes literally) say yes to it. In other words, if someone on stage turns to you and says, "Doctor, why does my baby have two heads?" you should respond with something like, "Because two heads are better than one."

Real life is like improv: the script's always changing, and saying yes keeps you in the flow, pulls for creativity, and makes it more fun. Try saying no out loud or in your mind. How's that feel? Then say yes. Which one feels better, opens your heart more, and draws you more into the world?

Saying yes to some part of life—to a condition or situation, to a relationship, to your history or personality, or to something happening inside your own mind—does not necessarily mean that you *like* it. You can say yes to pain, to sorrow, to the things that aren't going well for you or others.

Your yes means that you accept the facts as they are, that you are not resisting them emotionally even if you are trying with all your might to change them. This will usually bring some peace—and will help any actions you take be more effective.

How

Say yes to something you like. Then yes to something neutral. Both of these are probably easy.

Then say yes to something you don't like. Can you do that, too? As you do this, try to feel a sense that you are okay, fundamentally, even though what you dislike exists. Also try to feel some acceptance in your yes, some surrender to the facts as they are, whether you like them or not.

Try saying yes to more things that are not your preference. You're not saying yes that you approve of them, but —for example—yes it's raining at my picnic, yes people are poor and hungry across the planet, yes my career has stalled, yes I miscarried, yes my dear friend has cancer. Yes that's the way it is. Yes to being in traffic. Yes to the job you have. Yes to the body you have.

Yes to the twists and turns in your life so far: large and small; good, bad, and indifferent; past, present, and future. Yes to the younger sibling whose birth toppled you from your throne. Yes to your parents' work and your family circumstances. Yes to your choices after leaving home. Yes to what you had for breakfast. Yes to moving someplace new. Yes to the person you are sleeping with—or yes to not sleeping with anyone. Yes to having children—or to not having them.

Say yes to what arises in the mind. Yes to feelings, sensations, thoughts, images, memories, desires. Yes even to things that need to be restrained—such as an angry impulse to hit something, undeserved self-criticism, or an addiction.

Say yes to *all* the parts of the people in your life. Yes to the love in your parents and also yes to the parts that bothered you. Yes to a friend's flakiness amidst her good humor and patience, yes to another friend's sincerity amidst her irritability and criticalness. Yes to every bit of a child, a relative, a distant acquaintance, an adversary.

And yes to different parts of yourself—whatever they are. Not picking and choosing right now, but saying yes—YES—to whatever is inside you.

Play with different tones of yes (out loud or in your mind) related to different things—including the ones you don't like—and see how this feels. Try a cautious yes, as well as a yes that is confident, soft, rueful, or enthusiastic.

Feel your yes in your body. To adapt a method from Thich Nhat Hanh: Breathing in, feel something positive; breathing out, say yes. Breathe in energy, breathe out yes. Breathe in calm, breathe out yes.

Say yes to your needs. Yes to the need for more time to yourself, more exercise, more love, fewer sweets, and less anger. Try saying no to these needs in your mind or out loud, and see how that feels. And then say yes to them again.

Say yes to actions. To this kiss this lovemaking this reaching for the salt this brushing of teeth this last good-bye to someone you love.

Notice your nos. And then see what happens if you say yes to some of the things you've previously said no to.

Say yes to being alive. Yes to life. Yes to your own life. Yes to each year, each day. Yes to each minute.

Imagine that life is whispering yes. Yes to all beings, and yes to you. Everything you've said yes to is saying yes to you. Even the things you've said no to are saying yes to you!

Each breath, each heartbeat, each surge across a synapse: each one says yes. Yes, all yes, all saying yes.

Yes.

14

Take More Breaks

As we evolved in hunter-gatherer bands over millions of years, life moved at the pace of a walk, in rhythm with the seasons and with the rising and setting of the sun each day. In many of the hunter-gatherer cultures still existing today, it takes only a few hours a day to find food and shelter. It's a good guess that our ancient ancestors lived similarly, and spent the rest of their time relaxing, hanging out with friends, and looking at the stars.

Sure, life was tough in other ways, like dodging saber-tooth tigers, yet the point remains that the human body and mind evolved to be in a state of rest or leisure—in other words, *on a break*—much of the time.

But now, in the twenty-first century, people routinely work ten, twelve, or more hours a day—when you count commuting, working from home, and business travel—to put bread on the table and a roof over their heads. Much the same is true if a person is a stay-at-home parent, since "the village it takes to raise a child" usually looks more like a ghost town these days. Many of us are on the job and on the go from soon after we wake up in the morning and check e-mails or feed children (or both!) to the last time we pull phone messages at night.

It makes you wonder who is "advanced" and who is "primitive"!

The modern, pedal-to-the-metal lifestyle produces chronic stress and tension, and related physical and mental health issues. It also crowds out creative pursuits, friendships, recreation, spiritual life, and time for children and mates. As a therapist, I often see families where one or both parents are dealing with work sixty-plus hours a week; the job is an elephant in the living room, pushing everything else to the margins.

Imagine for a moment that you are sitting comfortably somewhere in your old age and looking back on your life and reflecting. Do you think you are going to wish you had spent more time on the job or doing housework?

Or wish you had spent more time relaxing, hanging out with friends, and looking at the stars?

How

So promise yourself that you'll take more breaks. Most of them will be brief, even a minute or less. But their accumulating effects will be really good for you.

Here are some methods for getting more breaks; pick the one(s) you like best:

- **Give yourself permission**—Tell yourself that you have worked hard and deserve a little rest; that it's important for your health; that your productivity will actually increase with more breaks; that even cavemen/women got more breaks than you!

- **Renounce everything else**—When it's time for a break, drop everything else for that time. Truly "clock out."

- **Take lots of microbreaks**—Many times a day, step out of the stream of doingness for at least a few seconds: close your eyes for a moment; take a couple of deep breaths; shift your visual focus to the farthest point you can see; repeat a saying or prayer; stand up and move about.

- **Shift gears**—Maybe you have to keep grinding through your To Do list, but at least take a break from task A by doing a different kind of task B.

- **Get out**—Look out the window; go outside and stare up at the sky; find a reason to walk out of a meeting.

- **Unplug**—If only for a few minutes, stop answering your phone(s); shut down e-mails; turn off the TV or radio; take off the earphones.

- **Make your body happy**—Wash your face; eat a cookie; smell something good; stretch; lie down; rub your eyes or ears.

- **Go on a mental holiday**—Remember or imagine a setting (mountain lake? tropical beach? grandma's kitchen?) that makes you feel relaxed and happy. When you can, go there and enjoy yourself. As I've told myself in certain situations, "They may have my body, but they don't get my mind."

- **Keep your stress needle out of the red zone**—If you find yourself getting increasingly frustrated or tense in some situation, disengage and take a break before your head explodes. Staying out of "red zone" stress is a serious priority for your long-term health and well-being.

To get at the underlying causes of your busy life and lack of breaks, consider all the things you think you have to do. Can you drop or delegate some of these? And can you take on fewer commitments and tasks in the future?

Personally, I've been slowly learning how to say no. No to low priority activities, no to great things I just don't have time for, no to my appetite for filling up my calendar.

Saying no will help you say yes to your own well-being, to friends, to activities that really feed you, to an uncluttered mind. To the stars twinkling high above your head.

15
Be Glad

In order to keep our ancestors alive in harsh and often lethal settings, neural networks evolved that continually look for, react to, store, and recall bad news—both "out there," in your environment, and "in here," inside your own head.

As a consequence, we pay a lot of attention to threats, losses, and mistreatment in our environment—and to our emotional reactions, such as worry, sadness, resentment, disappointment, and anger. We also focus on our own mistakes and flaws—and on the feelings of guilt, shame, inadequacy, and even self-hatred that get stirred up.

There's a place for noticing and dealing with things that could harm you or others. And a place for improving your own mind and character.

But because of the negativity bias of the brain, most of us go way overboard.

Which is really *unfair*. It's not fair to zero in on a bit of bad news and ignore or downplay all the good news around it. The results of that unfairness include uncalled-for anxiety, pessimism, blue moods, and self-doubt. Emphasizing the bad news also primes us to be untrusting or cranky with others.

But if you compensate for the brain's bias by actively looking for good news—especially the little things you are *glad* about—then you will feel happier, more at peace with the world, more open to others, and more willing to stretch for your dreams. And as your growing gladness naturally lowers your stress, you'll likely get physical health benefits as well, such as a stronger immune system.

Now, that's good news . . . about good news!

How

Look for things to be glad about, like:

- Bad things that never happened, or were not as bad as you feared

- Relief that hard or stressful times are over

- Good things that have happened to you in the past

- Good things in your life today, such as: friends, loved ones, children, pets, the health you have, stores stocked with food, public libraries, electricity, positive aspects of your work and finances, activities you enjoy, sunsets, sunrises . . . ice cream!

  Good things about yourself, such as positive character traits and intentions

Sink into feelings of gladness:

  "Glad" means "pleased with" or "happy about." So notice what it feels like—in your emotions, body, and thoughts—to be *pleased* with something or *happy* about it. When you create a clear sense-memory of a positive mental state, you can find your way back to it again.

  Be aware of small, subtle, mild, or brief feelings of gladness.

  Stay with the good news. Don't change the channel so fast!

  Notice if your feelings of gladness get hijacked by doubt or worry. Also be honest with yourself, and consider if you are kind of attached to your resentments, grievances, or "case" about other people. It's okay if it's hard for you to stay with gladness; it's really common. Just try to name to yourself what has happened in your mind—such as "hijacking" . . . "brooding" . . . "grumbling"— and then freely decide if you want to spiral down into the bad news, or if you want to focus on good news instead. Make a conscious decision, acknowledge it to yourself, and then act upon it.

- ◦{ Sometime every day, before going to bed, name to yourself at least three things you are glad about.

Share your feelings of gladness:

- ◦{ Make a point of mentioning to others something that you are pleased or happy about (often the little stuff of everyday life).

- ◦{ Look for opportunities to tell another person what you appreciate about him or her.

16

Have Faith

Try a little experiment: in your mind or out loud, complete this sentence a few times: "I have faith in _____ ." Then complete another sentence a few times: "I have no faith in _____ ." What do faith—and no faith—feel like?

In your experience of faith, there's probably a sense of *trusting* in something—which makes sense since the word comes from the Latin root, "to trust." ("Faith" can also mean a religion, but my meaning here is more general.) Faith feels good. To have confidence is to have faith; "con+fide" means "with+faith."

Faith comes from direct experience, reason, trusted sources, and sometimes from something that just feels deeply right and that's all you can say about it. You could have faith in both biological evolution and heaven. Sometimes faith seems obvious, like expecting water to yield each time you prepare to dive in; other times, faith is more of a conscious choice—an act of faith—such as choosing to believe that your child will be all right as he or she leaves home for college.

What do you have faith in—out there in the world or inside yourself?

For example, I have faith in the sun coming up tomorrow, my partner while rock climbing, science and scholarship, the kindness of strangers, the deliciousness of peaches, the love of my wife, God, and the desire of most people to live in peace. And faith in my determination, coffee-making skills, and generally good intentions.

In your brain, faith (broadly defined to include assumptions and expectations) is an efficient way to conserve neural resources by not figuring things out each time from scratch. The visceral sense of conviction in faith integrates prefrontal logic, limbic emotion, and brainstem arousal.

Without faith in the world and in yourself, life feels shaky and scary. Faith grounds you in what's reliable and supportive; it's the antidote to doubt and fear. It strengthens you and supports you in weathering hard times. It helps you stay on your chosen paths, with confidence they will lead to good places. Faith fuels the hope and optimism that encourage the actions that lead to the results that confirm your faith, in a lovely positive cycle. Faith lifts your eyes to the far horizons, toward what's sacred, even Divine.

How

Sure, some skepticism is good. But going overboard with it leads to an endless loop of mistrusting the world and doubting yourself. You need to have faith that you'll make good choices about where to have faith! Which means avoiding two pitfalls:

- Putting too much trust in the *wrong* places, such as in people who won't come through for you, in a business or job that's unlikely to turn out well, in dogmas and prejudices, or in a habit of mind that harms you—like a guardedness with others that may have worked okay when you were young but is now like walking around in a suit of armor that's three sizes too small.

- Putting too little trust in the *right* places, such as in the willingness of most people to hear what you really have to say, in the results that will come if you keep plugging away, or in the goodness inside your own heart.

So, first make a list of what you *do* have faith in—both in the world and in yourself. You can do this in your mind, on paper, or by talking with someone.

Next, ask yourself where your faith might be misplaced—in dry wells or in dogs that won't hunt. Be sure to consider too much faith in certain aspects of your own mind, such as in beliefs that you are weak or tainted, that others don't care about you, or that somehow you're going to get different results by doing pretty much the same old things.

Then pick one instance of misguided faith, and consciously step away from it: reflect on how you came to develop it and what it has cost you; imagine the benefits of a life without it; and develop a different resource to replace it. Repeat these steps for other cases of misplaced faith.

Second, make another list, this one of what you *could* reasonably have faith in—in the world and in yourself. These are missed opportunities for confidence—such as in people who could be trusted more (including children), in the basic safety of most days for most people, and in your own strengths and virtues.

Then pick one and see if you can have more faith in it. Remember the good reasons for relying upon it. Imagine how more trust in it will help you and others. Consciously choose to believe in it.

Third, consider some of the good qualities and aspirations in your innermost heart. Give yourself over to them for a moment—or longer. What's that like?

Try to have more faith in the best parts of yourself. They've always been faithful to you.

17

Find Beauty

Beauty is that which *delights* the senses—including the "sixth sense" of the mind.

Different people find beauty in different forms and places. You don't have to go to a museum, listen to a symphony, or eat a gourmet meal to be in the presence of beauty.

For example, here are some of the (maybe strange) things I find beautiful: A clump of grass in a sidewalk crack. The horn of a train as it moves away. The smell of cinnamon. The curve of highway cloverleafs. Kitchen knives. The faces of nurses. Courage. Falling water. A glazed donut. The touch of cashmere. Foam. Frisbees. Snakes. Geometrical proofs. Worn pennies. The feeling of catching a football.

What are some things that are beautiful to you?

There's so much beauty all around us. But I think that for many people, there is little sense of this. That was certainly true for me before I started deliberately looking for beauty. And then we wonder why life doesn't seem very delightful!

What do you feel when you encounter beauty, including in its everyday forms? Perhaps your heart opens, something eases in the mind, there's pleasure, and your spirits lift. The experience of beauty relieves stress, nourishes hope, and reminds us that there's much more to life than grinding through tasks. The sense of beauty can also be shared—have you ever admired a sunset with a friend?—bringing you closer to others.

How

Take a few moments each day to open to beauty. Really *look* at the things around you—particularly at the ordinary things we tend to tune out, such as the sky, appliances, grass, cars, weeds, familiar views, bookshelves, or sidewalks. Try the same with everyday sounds, smells, tastes, and touches. Also seek out lovely memories, feelings, or ideas.

Hunt for beauty like a child looking for seashells on a bountiful beach. Be open to things outside the frame of "nice" or "pretty." Let yourself be surprised. Find beauty in unexpected places.

When you find beauty, feel it. Open to a growing sense of boundless beauty above and below and stretching in all directions, like you're floating in a sea of rose petals.

Recognize the beauty in others, in their character, choices, sacrifices, aspirations. Understand the beauty in noble failures, quiet determination, leaps of insight, and joy at the good fortune of others. Hear the beauty of a parent's voice soothing a child, of friends laughing, of the click and clack of a teacher's chalk on the blackboard. See the beauty in the face of someone at the very beginning of this life, and see it in the face of someone at the very end.

Recognize the beauty in your own heart. Don't duck this one: as others are beautiful, so are you.

Make beauty with your hands, your words, and your actions.

Even the breath is beautiful. Breathing in beauty, let beauty breathe you.

18

Be Grateful

We experience gratitude when we are freely given something good.

Therefore, looking for opportunities for gratitude—developing an "attitude of gratitude"—is a great way to notice and enjoy some of the gifts you've received.

Gratitude does not mean ignoring difficulties, losses, or injustice. It just means *also* paying attention to the offerings that have come your way. Especially the little ones of everyday life.

When you do this, you're resting your mind increasingly on good things moving toward you, on being supported, on feelings of fullness—on the sense of having an open heart that moves toward an open hand.

Fuller and fuller, more and more fed by life instead of drained by it, you naturally feel like you have more of value inside yourself and more to offer to others.

And that is a very good thing. For example, studies by Robert Emmons and others have shown that gratitude is associated with greater well-being, better coping, and even better sleep (McCullough et al. 2001).

How

Prime your pump by bringing to mind someone you naturally feel grateful toward. Perhaps a friend, parent or grandparent, teacher, spiritual being, or pet.

Next, *look around and notice*, both here and now, and in the past:

- The gifts of the physical world, including the stars in the sky, the colors of the rainbow, and the remarkable fact that the seemingly arbitrary constants that determine how atoms stick together in our universe are just right for planets to form and life to develop—enabling you to be here today

- The gifts of nature, like the flight of a bird, the creatures that die so we may live, and your amazing brain

- The gifts of life, including the marvelous instructions for building a human being woven into the strands of DNA

- The gifts of nurturance, helpfulness, good counsel, and love from other people

These gifts are freely offered; no one can possibly earn them. All we can do is be grateful for these gifts, and do what we can in our own little corner of the world to use them well each day.

Let yourself *accept* these gifts. It would be rude—ungrateful!—to refuse them.

Remember that gratitude is not guilt or indebtedness —both of which actually make it harder to feel grateful. You may feel moved to be generous in turn—including in new directions, such as giving to some out of appreciation for what you have been given by others—but it will come from large-heartedness, not because you think you owe something. Gratitude moves us away from let's-make-a-deal exchanges in relationships toward a sense of abundance, in which you feel fed beyond measure and in turn give with all your heart without keeping score.

Then *recognize the benefits* to you of what has been given. Reflect on how it helps you and those you care about, makes you feel good, and fuels your own generosity in turn.

And *recognize the benevolence of the giver*, whether it is a person, Mother Nature, or the physical universe—or, if this is meaningful to you, something Divine. Don't minimize the benevolence to avoid feeling unworthy or indebted; open up to it as a telling of the truth, as a giving back to the giver, and as a joyful leaning toward that which is truly gift-giving in your world.

Last, *soak up the gifts coming to you*, whatever they are. Let them become part of you, woven into your body, brain, and being. As you inhale, as you relax, as you open, take in the good that you've been given.

19
Smile

Smiling has many benefits:

- Thinking of things that make you smile—like people you love, silly moments, stupid pet tricks, funny movies—helps you feel better right on the spot. Plus it calms down the stress response and releases wholesome neurochemicals like dopamine and natural opioids (e.g., endorphins).

- Researchers have found that the facial movements of smiling—independent of what a person actually feels inside—prompt the person to evaluate the world more positively (Niedenthal 2007).

- Smiling and the good feelings it encourages promote *approach behaviors*, a fancy term for paying more attention to the opportunities around you, going after your dreams with more confidence, and reaching out to others.

- ❧ Through what's called *emotional contagion*, when you smile and thus feel and act better, that influences others to feel and act better, too. Then nice positive cycles start rolling through a group—perhaps a family, a team at work, or simply a bunch of friends—in which your smile gets others to smile and be more positive, which snowballs into an even bigger grin for you.

- ❧ When you smile—authentically, to be sure, not in a false or Dr. Evil sort of way—that tells people you are not a threat, which calms the ancient, evolutionary tendency to be wary of others, and thus inclines them to be more open to you.

How

This is definitely *not* about putting a happy shiny face on depression, grief, fear, or anger. Smiling then would be phony, and would probably feel awful. But when you feel neutral or experience mild well-being, shifting into a small smile while thinking of good facts that make it real can naturally lift your mood and help you act more effectively.

So, in your mind or on paper, make a list of things that make you smile. Several times a day, look for moments to bring that list to mind . . . and a soft smile to your face.

Then notice the results, in how you feel inside, and in how you act toward others and how they respond to you. Savor these good feelings and successes, taking them in.

Smiling a few more times each day may not seem like much, but it will send wonderful ripples through your brain, body, mind, and relationships.

Now, isn't that something to smile about?

20
Get Excited

Excitement is energy plus positive emotion, and it is part of joy, passion, and having fun. It may be mild—but it still moves your needle. For example, on my personal 0-10 "thrillometer," seeing the stars on a clear night is about a 2 while the San Francisco Giants winning the World Series in 2010 was a 10.

When you consider excitement in this expanded way, what moves your own needle, even a little bit? How about the sound of bagpipes, a child's first steps, traveling some-place new, finishing a project that's gone well, dancing, laughing, finding something you've wanted on super-sale, or hearing a neat idea?

Of course it's hard, if not impossible, to feel excitement if you are ill or psychologically burdened. The inability to get excited is a sign that something's not right.

But under normal conditions, without excitement about *something*, life feels flat, bland, and inert. Passion helps ignite and sustain creativity, entrepreneurship, political action, and committed relationships. Getting excited about something *together* is bonding; shared enthusiasm makes a movie, concert, political rally, conversation, or lovemaking a lot more rewarding.

As you grew up, your natural liveliness may have been criticized, dampened, or squelched. In particular, passion is woven into both strong emotions and sex; if either of these has been shamed or numbed, so has excitement. Did any of this happen to you? If it did, then gradually making more room for passion in your life—more room for delight, eagerness, and energy—is a joyful way to express yourself more fully.

How

Find something that excites you, even just a bit. Feel the enjoyment in it. See if you can intensify the experience through a quick inhalation, a sense perhaps of energy rising in your body. Lift your chest and head, and let more aliveness come into your face. Register this feeling of excitement, and make room for it in your body. Then as you go through your day, notice what moves your own thrillometer, particularly in subtle ways. Look for things to get excited about!

Tell yourself that it's okay to get excited, thrilled, or aroused. Take a stand for a life that's got some juiciness in it. Reflect on your passions as a younger person: What's happened to them? Should you dust one of them off and recommit to it?

Pick a part of your life that's become static, perhaps stale—such as cooking, a job, housework, repetitive parts of parenting, even sex—and really pursue ways to pep it up. Try new dishes, turn up the music, get goofy, dance with the baby, vary your routines, and so on.

Be aware of how you might be putting a damper on excitement, such as tightening your body, deadening your feelings, or murmuring thoughts like *Don't stand out . . . Don't be "too much" for people . . . Don't be uncool.* As you become more mindful of the wet blankets in your own mind, they'll dry out.

Consider some of the practices for raising energy from yoga, martial arts, or other forms of physical training. These include taking multiple deep breaths (not to the point of lightheadedness), sensing energy in the core of your body a few inches below the navel, jumping up and down a few times, making deep guttural sounds (don't try this at work!), or visualizing bright light.

Join with the excitement of others. Focus on something that lights up a friend or your partner, and look for things that could be fun, enlivening, or interesting about it for *you*. Don't fake anything, but nudge your own energy upwards; get more engaged with the other person's passion, which may ignite your own.

Don't rain on other people's parade—and don't let them rain on yours. Sure, if you're getting too revved up, read the social signals and either dial down your energy or take it elsewhere. But be aware that excitement makes some people uncomfortable—to keep their own passions bottled up, they put a lid on those of others—and honestly, that's their problem, not yours. With this sort of person, you may need to disengage, find others who share your interests, and walk to the beat of your own drummer.

For me, the essence of excitement is *enthusiasm*—whose root meaning is quite profound: "moved by something extraordinary, even divine."

part three:

Build Strengths

21
Find Strength

To make your way in life—to enjoy the beautiful things it offers, to steer clear of hazards and protect yourself and others, and find friendship and love—you need strength. Not chest-thumping pushiness, but determination and grit.

Strength comes in many forms, including endurance, losing on the little things in order to win on the big ones, and restraint. For example, if you want to move a boat at the edge of a dock, don't run into it with a big smash; you'll just hurt yourself. Instead, stand on the edge of the dock, put your hand on the boat, and lean into it. *Strength keeps leaning.*

Inner strength is not all or nothing. You can build it, just like a muscle.

How

Mental strength draws on physical health, which is fueled by: eating protein at every meal; taking vitamin and mineral supplements daily; exercising several times a week; setting aside seven to nine hours a day for sleep; using intoxicants in moderation or not at all; and addressing and resolving chronic health problems, even seemingly mild ones. If you are not doing these, how about starting today?

Make a list of your strengths, such as intelligence, honesty, bearing pain, natural talents, recognizing good in others, or just surviving. Be accurate—not unfairly self-critical. Recognizing your strengths will help you feel stronger. If it's appropriate, ask someone what he or she thinks some of your strengths are.

Think about some of the good things you use your strengths for, such as earning a living, raising a family, growing as a person, or making our world better. Tell yourself, *It is good for me to be strong. My strength helps good things happen. Good people want me to be strong; anyone who wants me to be weak is not on my side.* Notice any beliefs that it is bad to be strong . . . and then turn your attention back to the good reasons for being strong.

To increase your sense of strength, recall times you felt strong. (For me, many of these have involved standing up for others, or physical activities like hiking in wilderness.) What did your body feel like then? What was your posture, point of view, or intention? Explore embodying strength right now: maybe lifting your chin, widening your stance, or breathing deeply. Take in these physical sensations and attitudes of strength so you can tap into them again.

Notice how good it feels to be strong. Feel the pleasure in your body, perhaps a quiet fierceness and resolve. Enjoy the confidence that strength brings, the sense of possibility. Appreciate how your strength empowers your caring, protectiveness, and love.

Tell yourself that you are strong. That you can endure, persist, cope, and prevail. That you are strong enough to hold your experience in awareness without being overwhelmed. That the winds of life can blow, and blow hard, but you are a deeply rooted tree, and winds just make you even stronger.

And when they are done blowing, there you still stand. Offering shade and shelter, flowers and fruit. Strong and lasting.

22
Be Mindful

As we saw in the introduction to this book, the movements of information through your nervous system—which is what I mean by "mental activity," most of which is unconscious—can create lasting changes in brain structure: "neurons that fire together, wire together." In particular, this rewiring is accelerated for what's in the field of focused attention. In effect, attention is like a combination spotlight and vacuum cleaner: it illuminates what it rests upon and then sucks it into your brain.

Since attention is largely under volitional control—you can direct it with conscious effort—you have an extraordinary tool at your disposal all day long to gradually sculpt your brain in positive ways. Unfortunately, most people do not have very good control of their attention: it's hard for them to rest it where they want and keep it there—such as an important but boring meeting, or the sensations of one breath after another—and hard to pull it away from things that aren't helpful, like senseless worry, self-critical rumination, or too much TV. The reasons include temperament (for example, anxious, spirited), personal history (for example, losses or traumas that keep them on edge), and our hyper-stimulating, ADD-ish culture.

Happily, attention is very trainable. You really can develop better control of your spotlight/vacuum cleaner. This is where mindfulness comes in—which simply means being steadily aware of something. As you practice being mindful, you will gain more control over your attention.

You could be mindful of what's around you—perhaps key details at work, the deeper wants of your partner, flowers blooming and children smiling, or where you left the car keys. You could also be mindful of your inner world, such as soft feelings of hurt underneath brittle anger, your good intentions and basic decency, or unrealistic expectations that set you up for disappointment.

Mindfulness has lots of benefits. It brings important information about what's happening around you and inside you. It helps you witness your experience without being swept away by it, and to hold it in a larger context; as your mindful awareness increases, negative experiences have less impact on you. And the duration and intensity of what you are paying attention to tends to increase its traces in your brain. Consequently, mindfulness really helps you take in positive experiences.

To some extent, mindfulness has become associated with Buddhism, but all the world's religions and moral traditions value being mindful—rather than mindless!

Additionally, mindfulness is increasingly taught in secular settings such as hospitals, corporations, classrooms, professional sports, and military training.

Studies have shown that regular practices of mindfulness:

- Thicken cortical layers in regions of the brain that control attention (so you get better at attention itself) (Lazar et al. 2005)

- Add neural connection in the insula, a part of the brain that supports both self-awareness and empathy for the emotions of others (Lazar et al. 2005)

- Increase the relative activation of the left prefrontal cortex (behind the left side of your forehead), which helps control and reduce negative emotions (Davidson 2004)

- Strengthen your immune system (Davidson et al. 2003)

- Reduce the impact of pain and accelerate postsurgical recovery (Kabat-Zinn 2003; Kabat-Zinn, Lipworth, and Burney 1985)

Pretty great for a simple method—mindfulness—that you can use, privately and effectively, anywhere you go.

How

Mindfulness is natural. You are already mindful of many things each day. The problem is that most of us remain mindful for only a few seconds at a time. The trick is to have more "episodes" of mindfulness, and to lengthen and deepen them.

So, set aside a minute or more every day to be deliberately mindful—focusing on a specific object of attention (e.g., the sensations of breathing) or opening wide to whatever moves through awareness. You could extend these moments of mindfulness into a longer period of meditation, letting your mind become increasingly clear and peaceful.

Then, throughout the day, add some additional times of mindfulness when you remain stably present with whatever is happening around you and inside you. If you like, use recurring events such as meals, a telephone ringing, or walking through a doorway as reminders to be mindful.

It will support and deepen your mindfulness to bring an attitude of curiosity, openness, non-judgmental acceptance, and even a kind of friendliness to the things you're aware of. Also try to develop a background awareness of how mindful you are being; in effect, you are paying attention . . . to attention, in order to get better at it.

These practices will gradually train your brain to be more mindful, which will bring you many rewards. For as William James—the first major American psychologist— wrote over a century ago (1890, p. 424): "The faculty of voluntarily bringing back a wandering attention, over and over again, is the very root of judgment, character, and will ... An education which should improve this faculty would be *the* education *par excellence*."

23
Be Patient

It's fine to want things to happen in a proper and timely way. But what if you need to hang in there for several years in your current job before you can move on to a better one, or you're stuck on hold listening to elevator music, going to the mailbox each day for a long-awaited letter, or trying to get a squirming toddler into a car seat? Now what?

Patience means handling delay, difficulty, or discomfort without getting aggravated. Circumstances are what they are, but patience protects you from their impact like a shock absorber.

In contrast, impatience interprets circumstances as you being hindered or mistreated, so you feel frustrated, let down, or annoyed. Then insistence comes in: "This must change!" But by definition you can't fulfill that commandment (otherwise, there'd be nothing to get impatient about). Impatience combines all three ingredients of toxic stress: unpleasant experiences, pressure or urgency, and lack of control.

Impatience with others contains implicit criticism and irritation—and people want to get away from both of these. Just recall how you feel when someone is impatient with you. Or consider how others react when you are impatient with them.

Impatience is dissatisfaction; it is resistance to the way it is. Patience senses a fundamental alrightness, the doorway to contentment. Impatience is angry; patience is peaceful. Impatience narrows down onto what's "wrong," while patience keeps you wide open to the big picture. Impatience can't stand unpleasant feelings; patience helps you tolerate physical and emotional discomfort. Impatience wants rewards *now*; patience helps you tolerate delayed gratification, which fosters increased success and sense of worth.

Patience may seem like a superficial virtue, but actually it embodies a deep insight into the nature of things: they're intertwining, messy, imperfectible, and usually not about you. Patience also contains a wonderful teaching about desire: wish for something, sure, but be at peace when you can't have it. Patience knows you can't make the river flow any faster.

How

For an overview, reflect on these questions:

- ◄ What does patience feel like? Impatience?

- ◄ How do you feel about someone who's really patient? And about someone who's really impatient?

- ◄ What makes you impatient?

- ◄ What helps you stay patient?

In challenging situations:

- ◄ Try to step back from thoughts that make you impatient, such as righteousness, superiority, or insistence. Remember that standards differ among persons and cultures. Remind yourself that there is (usually) nothing truly urgent.

- ◄ Be aware of any body sensations or emotions triggered by delay or frustration—and see if you can tolerate them without reacting with impatience. Relax your body, come into the present moment, and open to feeling that you are basically all right right now.

- ◄ Rather than feeling that you are "wasting" time, find things that are rewarding in situations that try your patience; for example, look around and find something beautiful. Pay attention to your breath while relaxing your body, and wish others well. Similarly, rather than viewing yourself as "waiting in" situations, explore the sense of "being in" them. Enjoy the time being.

- ❧ Try to have compassion for others who seem to be in the way or taking too long. For example, a pet peeve of mine is people who stand in the middle of public doorways, but lately I've been realizing they have no idea they're blocking others.

- ❧ Pick a conversation—or even a relationship altogether—and deliberately bring more patience to it. You could react more slowly and thoughtfully (and never interrupt), let the other person have more time to talk, and allow minor issues to slide by.

- ❧ Play with routine situations—such as a meal— and take a few extra seconds or minutes before starting, in order to strengthen your patience muscles.

- ❧ Offer patience as a *gift*—to others, dealing with their own issues, and to yourself, wanting true happiness. Life is like a vast landscape with both soft grass and sharp thorns; impatience rails at the thorns; patience puts on a pair of shoes.

24
Enjoy Humility

Some might think that humility means being less than others, a doormat, second-class, or self-effacing.

But actually, it's none of these. *Humility* just means that you're stepping out of the rat race of self-glorification. You're not trying to build up your ego, impress people, or compete with others for status. You're not preoccupied with yourself. What a relief!

The root of the word "humble," comes from the Latin for "ground." With humility, you abide like the earth itself: solid, unpretentious, creating value without fanfare.

Humility is not humiliation. In fact, relaxed humility builds your confidence: you know your intentions are honorable, and you expect that others will probably be supportive.

In relationships, humility creates comfort and ease. It's like an open hand, empty of the weapons of superiority, scorn, or self-importance. You're receptive to others, not presuming your own infinite wisdom; as a result, they're less likely to feel criticized, and less likely to get defensive or competitive with you. Not chasing praise, you become more aware of your natural worth—which becomes easier for others to see as well; the less you focus on being appreciated, the more appreciation you'll get.

Humility embodies wisdom. It recognizes that everyone, including the grandest, is humbled by needing to depend on a vast web—of people, technology, culture, nature, sunlight, and biochemistry—to live a single day. Fame is soon forgotten. At the end of it all, we're each reduced to dust. Humility helps you be at peace with these facts.

How

Healthy humility is grounded in healthy self-worth. Feeling humble does *not* mean feeling inadequate. If you're like me and self-worth has been an issue, take steps over time to deepen your felt recognition of your own good qualities with the practices of *taking in the good* and *seeing the good in yourself* (chapters 2 and 5). Be mindful of any challenges to self-worth that could lead you to compensate with overconfidence, puffing up your reputation, or preemptive strikes of superiority.

Nor does being humble mean tolerating mistreatment. Speak up and do what you can. Knowing that you are prepared to be assertive makes it easier to relax into the unguardedness of humility.

A humble person wishes all beings well—including oneself. You can still dream big dreams (chapter 40) and help them come true. With humility, you pursue excellence, not fame.

Be honest with yourself about any ways you are *not* humble, any times you've been cocky, pretentious, promoting yourself with exaggerations, or entitled. In particular, try to catch any antihumility in your relationships, such as acting one-up or better-than, or being (even subtly) dismissive or devaluing. Instead, flow more with others: be modest, don't always try to win the point, don't interrupt, and don't claim more than your share of air time or credit.

In your brain, the background murmurings of self-centered preoccupations—*I sounded really good there . . . Hope they thought so . . . I wish people praised me more . . . I want to be special*—are supported by networks in the top middle portions of your cortex. When you step out of that stream and are simply present with what is, without turning it into a story about yourself, different networks come to the fore, on the sides (especially right) of your head (Farb et al. 2007). You can stimulate these networks and thus strengthen some of the neural substrates of humility by:

- Taking a panoramic, big-picture view of situations and your part in them

- Sensing your breath as a unified whole, with all the sensations of it appearing in awareness as a single gestalt (rather than attention skipping from sensation to sensation as it typically does)

Explore humility on a global scale. For example, notice any beliefs that your political viewpoint, nation, or spirituality is superior to that of others. Also consider your consumption of the planet's resources from the perspective of humility; are there any changes you'd like to make?

Throughout, be aware of the rewards of humility. Enjoy how it makes your day simpler, keeps you out of conflicts with others, and brings you peace.

25
Pause

Doing therapy with a child who's learning better self-control, sometimes I'll ask if he or she would like to ride a bike with no brakes. The answer—even from the most spirited ones—is always no. They understand that no brakes mean either a boring ride or a crash; paradoxically, brakes let you go fast and have the most fun.

It's the same in life. Whether you're faced with criticism at work, a partner whose feelings are hurt, an internal urge to lash out verbally, or an opportunity for some gratification that will cost you later, you've got to be able to put on the brakes for a moment—to *pause*. Otherwise, you'll likely crash, one way or another.

Your brain works through a combination of excitation and inhibition: gas pedals and brakes. Only about 10 percent of its neurons are inhibitory, but without their vital influence, it's your brain that would crash. For example, individual neurons that are over-stimulated will die, and seizures involve runaway loops of excitation.

In daily life, pausing provides you with the gift of time. Time to let other people have their say without feeling interrupted. Time for you to find out what's really going on, calm down and get centered, sort out your priorities, and craft a good response. Time both to bring cool reason to hot feelings, and to enable wholeheartedness to soften hard-edged positions. Time for the "better angels of your nature" to take flight in your mind.

How

Let yourself *not* act. Sometimes we get so caught up in neverending doing that it becomes a habit. Make it okay with yourself to simply *be* from time to time.

A few times a day, stop for a few seconds and tune in to what's going on for you, especially beneath the surface. Use this pause to make space for your experience, like airing out a long-closed closet into a big room. Catch up with yourself.

Before beginning a routine activity, take a moment to become fully present. Try this with meals, starting the car, brushing your teeth, taking a shower, or answering the phone.

After someone finishes speaking to you, take a little longer than usual before you reply. Let the weight of the other person's words—and more importantly, the person's underlying wants and feelings—really sink in. Notice how this pause affects you—and affects the other person's response to you.

If an interaction is delicate or heated, slow it down. You can do this on your own even if the other person keeps rat-a-tat-tatting away. Without being deliberately annoying, you could allow a few seconds more silence (or even longer) before you respond, or speak in a more measured way.

If need be, pause the interaction altogether by suggesting you talk later, calling time out, or (last resort) telling the other person you're done for now and hanging up the phone. In most relationships, you do not need the permission of the other person to end an interaction! Of course, pausing a conversation (which may have become an argument) midstream is more likely to go well if you also propose another, realistic time to resume.

Before doing something that could be problematic—like getting high, putting a big purchase on a credit card, firing off an irritated e-mail, or talking about person A to person B—stop and forecast the consequences. Try to imagine them in living color: the good, the bad, and the ugly. Then make your choice.

Last, for a minute or more each day, pause globally. Just sit, as a body relaxed and breathing. Letting thoughts and feelings come and go as they will, not chasing after them. Nowhere you need to go, nothing you need to do, no one you need to be. Paused from doing, sinking into being.

26
Have Insight

By *insight*, I mean understanding yourself, particularly how your mind constructs your reactions to things.

Let's say I've just come home from a frazzling day of work, and my wife gives me a hug and then asks in passing, "Did you get any eggs?" (which we had not discussed; I hadn't known we needed any)—and I get irritated, tense in my body, and a little sad. What's happening here?

Her casual, neutral question about the eggs—the *stimulus*—led to a *response* of irritation, tension, and sadness *due to* several factors at work in my mind: stress, a sensitivity to possible criticism (that I had forgotten the eggs) from growing up with a fault-finding (although very loving) mother, and my guilt about not doing enough housework. If those factors disappeared, so would my upset.

Recall a moderately irritating or worrying situation of your own: what were your reactions to it, and *why* were you reacting that way? Consider stress, fatigue, your temperament, how you interpret certain events, your history with the others involved, and the impact of your childhood.

As with everybody else, your reactions come from *causes* inside your mind. Therefore, if you can change the causes, you can change your reactions for the better:

- Seeing, in the moment, how your mind has colored your perceptions and turbocharged your emotions can transform your reactions—sometimes rapidly and dramatically, like waking up from a bad dream.

- Over time, you can gradually alter or get better control over the mental factors that wear on your well-being, relationships, and effectiveness.

How

Begin by shifting attention away from the external causes of your reactions—like what someone said to you—and toward the causes *inside your own mind,* such as how you interpret what was said, attribute intentions to the speaker, or feel especially prickly because of your history with that person.

The mind is like a great mansion, with cozy dens, dusty closets, and dank cellars. Insight explores it, opening closed doors and making sense of what it finds: sometimes a treasure chest, sometimes smelly old shoes—though truly, it's usually treasure, including your natural good-ness, sincere efforts, and lovingkindness.

Nonetheless, it can feel scary to look around (especially in those cellars); these suggestions could help you keep going:

- Remember the benefits of insight. For example, I'm very independent, so I remind myself that the main forces controlling me are actually inside my own head (e.g., beliefs left over from childhood); understanding them reduces their power over me.

- Bring to mind the feeling of being with someone who cares about you—like a friend walking with you down a dark street. As they say in AA: "The mind is a dangerous neighborhood; don't go in alone."

- Regard what you find without making it good or bad. It's not *you*. It's only a sensation, feeling, thought, or want arising in a room in your mind. Try to be accepting rather than self-critical, compassionate rather than shaming. Everybody, me included, has wild stuff in the mind; it's a jungle in there!

Drawing on the resources in the bullet points just above, look around inside your mind. Now sense beneath the surface and ask yourself one or more of these questions:

❧ What is softer—such as hurt, sadness, or fear—below hard and defended stuff like anger or justifications?

❧ What am I really wanting, deep down? What are the good desires underlying bad behaviors? Such as the normal desire for safety at the root of anxious rumination.

❧ What material here is from a time when I was younger? (For example, because I was often excluded from groups in school, I still sometimes feel like an outsider in groups when I'm really not.)

❧ What am I getting stuck on? Like fixating on a position or goal—or even a word. What am I trying to control that's not controllable (e.g., whether someone loves me)?

❧ How is my gender shaping my reactions? Or my temperament, cultural and ethnic background, or personality?

You can use these methods for insight on the fly, when things come up for you. And you can use them to drill down into a specific issue, such as sensitivity to criticism, longing for approval, tension with your parents, or efforts to get into a good relationship

Whatever you find, try to relax and open to it. Helpful or unhelpful, it's just furniture in the mansion of your mind.

27

Use Your Will

Life has challenges. To meet them, you need to be able to push through difficulties, stretch for other people, restrain problematic desires while pursuing wholesome ones, and do the hard thing when you must.

This means using your will.

We commonly equate will with willpower—the deliberate application of vigorous effort, such as lifting the last, strenuous rep of weight in a gym.

But will is a larger matter: it's a *context of commitment*, as for a mother devoted to the care of her family. Will is giving yourself over to your highest purposes, which lift you and carry you along. This kind of will feels like being pulled by inspiration rather than pushed by stubbornness. Surrendered rather than driven.

How

What does it actually mean, to make your highest purposes the engine of your life? As a framework for the answer, I'd like to draw on four qualities of a strongly dedicated person identified by the Buddha which have meant a lot to me personally: *ardent, resolute, diligent,* and *mindful.* Please consider how each of these could help you be more willful in one or more key areas, such as being braver in intimate relationships, completing your education, doing your fair share of housework, or sticking with a diet.

Ardent (a variation on ardor) means wholehearted, enthusiastic, and eager. Not dry, mechanical, or merely dogged. For example, why do you *care* about what happens in this aspect of your life, why does it *matter*? Let yourself be heartfelt and passionate about your aims and activities here.

Resolute means you are wholly committed and unwavering. Bring to mind an experience of absolute determination, such as a time you protected a loved one. You may feel a firming in the chest, a sense of every bit of you pulling for the same thing. Explore this feeling as it might apply to a particular part of your life. Imagine yourself staying resolute here as you face temptations—saying no, for example, to the donuts offered in a meeting—and take in the ways this would feel good to you. Get in touch with your resolve each morning, surrender to it, and let it guide you through the day.

Diligent means you are conscientious and thorough. Not as a grind, not from guilt or compulsion, but because—from the Latin root for "diligence"—you "love, take delight in" the stepping stones toward your higher purposes. This is where ardency and resolution often break down, so to help yourself:

- Keep in mind the reasons for your efforts; open to and try to feel their rewards, such as knowing that you are doing the best you can in the service of a good cause and deserve what's called "the bliss of blamelessness."

- Translate big purposes into small, doable daily actions. Don't let yourself get overwhelmed.

- Find the structures, routines, and allies that help you keep going.

- Tell the truth to yourself about what's actually happening. Are you doing what you had intended to do? If you're not, admit it to yourself. Then start over: re-find your wholehearted commitment, see what there is to do, and do it.

Mindful means that you know if you're being willful or lackadaisical. You're aware of your inner world, of the mental factors that block the will (e.g., self-doubt, lethargy, distractibility) and those that fuel it (e.g., enthusiasm, strength, grit, tenacity). You recognize if you've grown willful to a fault, caught up in purposes that are outdated or not worth their cost. You're able to make skillful course corrections that keep you aligned with your highest purposes.

Last, *enjoy* your will. Exercising it can get kind of grim if you're not careful. But actually, a person can be both lighthearted and strong-willed. Take pleasure in the strength in your will, and the fruits it brings you.

28
Take Refuge

In Hawaii one time, my wife Jan and I visited a "place of refuge." People fleeing for their lives could come there and be sheltered. Related customs exist around the world; for example, in medieval Europe, a person could take refuge in a church and be protected there.

Less formally, we all need everyday refuges from challenges, sorrows, and the occasional sheer craziness of the world. Otherwise, you get too exposed to the cold winds of life, and too drained by the daily round. Without refuge, after awhile you can feel like you're running on empty.

Refuges include people, places, memories, and ideas—anyone or anything that provides reliable sanctuary and protection, that's reassuring, comforting, and supportive, so you can let down your guard and gather strength and wisdom.

A refuge could be curling up in bed with a good book, having a meal with friends, or making a To Do list to organize your day. Or remembering your grandmother, feeling strength in your body, trusting the findings of science, talking with a trusted friend or counselor, having faith, or reminding yourself that although you're not rich, you're financially okay.

The world's religions also have refuges that may speak to you, such as sacred settings, texts, individuals, teachings, rituals, objects, and congregations.

Personally, one of my favorite refuges is *practice* itself: the theme of this book. It makes me feel good to trust that if I keep plugging away, then I can gradually become happier and more loving.

What gives you a sense of refuge?

How

Make a written or mental list of at least a few things that are refuges for you. And if you can, take a moment each day to consciously take refuge in those things.

You can "take refuge" in several ways:

- *Go to* a refuge

- *Come from* a refuge

- *Abide as* a refuge

- Sense a refuge *at work in your life*

Personally, it's been a breakthrough to imagine that my refuges already exist inside me, that I can live *from* them, as an expression of them in this life. When you take refuge in this way, you are giving yourself over to wholesome forces, and letting them work through you and carry you along.

You can take refuge explicitly, with words, by saying things in your mind like *I take refuge in* _____ . Or *I abide as* _____ . Or _____ *flows through me.*

Or just sense the refuge without words: feel what it is like for you to be in it, safe and supported, *home.*

Then repeat your way of taking refuge for each of your refuges. Try to do this every day, as soon as you remember to do so. It only takes a few minutes or less. And you can even do it in the middle of traffic or a meeting.

Once you have finished taking refuge, sense the good feelings and thoughts sinking deeply into you, filling you up, and weaving themselves into your being—a resource and inner light that you'll take with you wherever you go.

29

Risk the Dreaded Experience

When things happened to you as a child—or you saw them happening to others—you naturally formed expectations about what you'd likely feel in similar situations in the future. Based on these expectations, you developed responses: do *this* to get pleasure, do *that* to avoid pain. Then experiences in adulthood added additional, related expectations and responses.

Consequently, the following sequence routinely happens inside you, me, and everyone else many times a day—usually within a few seconds and often unconsciously:

1. A feeling or desire emerges in the mind, seeking expression.

2. This activates an associated expectation of emotional pain (from subtle unease to extreme

trauma) if the feeling or desire is expressed; this pain is the "dreaded experience."

3. This expectation triggers an inhibition of the original feeling or desire in order to avoid risking the dreaded experience.

For example, (1) you'd like more caring from someone, but (2) your childhood has led you to be cautious about revealing those vulnerable longings, so (3) you play it safe and don't ask for anything.

Take a moment to find one or more ways that this sequence—(1) an *emerging self-expression* leads to (2) an *associated expectation*, which leads to (3) an *inhibiting response*—unfolds in your mind. Here are some examples:

- (1) You want to get closer (e.g., emotionally, physically) to someone, but (2) moving closer exposes you to the risk of rejection, so (3) you do something that is distancing.

- (1) A feeling comes up (e.g., sadness, anger) but (2) expressing this feeling (or feelings in general) was discouraged in your childhood, so (3) you change the subject, make a joke, or otherwise move away from the emotion.

- (1) A desire arises to make something happen (e.g., aim for a new goal at work, write a song, plant a garden), but (2) you fear being unsuccessful, unsupported, scorned, or thwarted if you stick your neck out, so (3) you set aside your dream one more day.

Sometimes this is reasonable. For instance, (1) the urge to tell your boss to stuff it (2) prompts an expectation of big trouble if you do, (3) so you keep quiet.

But if you're like me and most people, your expectations of pain are often unreasonable. The negativity bias of the brain makes you overestimate both the likelihood of a bad outcome from self-expression and the amount of pain you'll feel if something bad actually happens. Further, the deep-down expectations that most shape self-expression developed when you were a child, so it is normal for them to be:

- Concrete, simplistic, and rigid—even though now you can think in more abstract, complex, and flexible ways

- Based on a time when you (a) were stuck with certain people (e.g., family members, peers), (b) had few resources, and (c) felt pain keenly—even though now you have much more (a) choice in your relationships, (b) assertiveness, money, and other resources, and (c) capacity to cope with pain.

These unreasonable expectations lead to responses that are needlessly pinched and cramped: we numb out internally, muzzle ourselves, stay safe and distant in relationships, and shrink our dreams. The experiences we dread hem us in, like taboo lands surrounding a shrinking little pasture, controlling us, telling us: "Don't chance that, live smaller." And most of the time, we suffer these costs without even realizing it.

What's the alternative?

It's to risk the dreaded experience—and reap the rewards that result. For example:

- ≼ (1) Wishing for something from an intimate partner, (2) you feel nervous about saying it, yet you know it's likely to be well-received and that you'll be fundamentally all right if it's not, so (3) you decide to speak up and risk feeling let down—and with some zigs and zags, it works out pretty well.

- ≼ (1) You don't feel your boss fully appreciates your abilities, but (2) he reminds you of your critical father and you dread those old feelings of hurt and low worth if you ask for more challenging (and interesting) assignments. So you plan carefully and identify a project he'll probably support, and you bring to mind, again and again, positive experiences of feeling seen and valued by others to help you cope if he is dismissive of you. (3) Having done your homework, you approach your boss with strength and clarity, which increases your odds of success.

- ≼ (1) You want to start a business. (2) Even though you worry about looking like a fool if it fails, you remind yourself that most people respect those who stick their necks out and have an entrepreneurial spirit. (3) So you start that business and do your best, at peace with whatever may happen.

How

Start by *observing* how this sequence proceeds in your mind: (1) self-expression → (2) expectation of pain → (3) inhibition. This is the most important step (which is why the explanation above is longer than usual). You'll frequently see it in retrospect, when you replay a response you had in a situation—a (3)—and realize that its *function* was to shut down your self-expression. At bottom, many of our reactions are strategies (often unconscious ones) for avoiding a dreaded experience.

Next, *challenge your expectations.* Are they really true? Help yourself appreciate the *fact* that expressing your emotions and wants—in reasonably skillful ways—will usually lead to good results. Speak to yourself like a wise, firm, and encouraging swim coach talking you through the first time you dove into a pool, with lines like *Other people have done this; it turned out okay for them and it can be the same for you. You have the abilities to make this work. Yes, it won't be perfect and might be uncomfortable, but you will be all right. I believe in you. Believe in yourself.*

Then, move out of your comfort zone by *taking calculated risks.* Start with easy situations in which the odds of self-expression causing a bad result are small—and even if the bad result were to occur, it would be only mildly uncomfortable for you. Then work your way up the ladder of increasingly vulnerable and high-stakes self-expression. A wonderful freedom grows in the heart as you do this; you're less cowed by dreaded experiences and not clipping your wings to avoid them. If a particular self-expression does lead to a painful result for you, notice that you can cope with this pain and that it soon comes to an end, and absorb the reasonable lessons (e.g., it's not wise to confide in a certain friend). Overall, you could well decide that it's worth occasionally feeling some pain in order to gain the much greater pleasures of fuller self-expression.

Last, *take it in* when you risk self-expression and it turns out fine (as it usually does). Really highlight it in your mind when pessimistic expectations don't come true, or when feared events do occur but they're not all that upsetting. Open to the satisfaction of expressing yourself, and let it sink in. Feel the healthy pride and self-respect earned by being brave enough to dive in.

30
Aspire without Attachment

To live is to pursue goals. Out of healthy self-interest and kindness to yourself, it's natural and fine to seek security, success, comfort, enjoyment, creative expression, physical and mental health, connection, respect, love, self-actualization, and spiritual development.

The question is whether you go after your goals with stress and drivenness—in a word, with *attachment*—or with outer effort and inner peacefulness, rewarded by the journey itself no matter the destination: with *aspiration*.

The difference between attachment and aspiration got really clear for me one time in Boulder, Colorado, where I'd gone with my old friend Bob for a week of rock climbing. Our guide, Dave, asked us what our goals were, and I said I wanted to climb 5.11 (a stiff grade) by the end of the week; at that point I could barely climb 5.8. Bob stared at me and then said this was crazy, that I'd only get frustrated and disappointed (Bob's pretty driven, and doesn't like falling short). I said no, that it would be a win for me either way: my goal was so ambitious that if I failed to reach it there'd be no shame, and if I did manage to fulfill it, wow, that would be a ton of fun. So I kept banging away, getting steadily better: 5.8, 5.9, easy 5.10, hard 5.10 . . . and then on the last day, I followed Dave without a fall on solid 5.11. Yay!

At the heart of attachment is *craving*—broadly defined—which contains and leads to many kinds of suffering (from subtle to intense). And while it may be an effective goad for a while—the stick that whips the horse into a lather—in the long run it is counterproductive, when that horse keels over. On the other hand, aspiration—working hard toward your goals without getting hung up on the results—feels good, plus it helps you stretch and grow without worrying about looking bad. Paradoxically, holding your goals lightly increases the chance of attaining them, while being attached—and thus fearing failure—gets in the way of peak performance.

If you sit on the couch your whole life and never take care of or go after anything important, you can avoid the pitfalls of attachment. But if you have a job, intimate relationship, family, service, art, or spiritual calling, the challenge is to stay firm in your course, with dedication and discipline, centered in aspiration.

How

Aspiration is about *liking,* while attachment is about *wanting*—and these involve separate systems in your brain (Berridge and Robinson 1998; Pecina, Smith, and Berridge 2006). Liking what is pleasant and disliking what is unpleasant are normal and not a problem. Trouble comes when we tip into the craving and strain inherent in wanting, wanting, wanting what's pleasant to continue and what's unpleasant to end. So learn to recognize the differences between liking and wanting in your body, emotions, attitudes, and thoughts. I think you'll find that liking feels open, relaxed, and flexible while wanting feels tight, pressed, contracted, and fixated.

Then, see if you can stay with liking without slipping into wanting:

- Help little alarm bells to go off in your mind— Alert! Caution!—when you get that familiar feeling of wanting/craving, especially when it's subtle and floating around in the back of your mind.

- Relax any sense of "gotta have it." Feel into the ways your life is and will be basically all right even if you don't attain a particular goal. Seek results from a place of fullness, not scarcity or lack.

- ❧ Try to remain relatively peaceful—even in the midst of passionate activity—since intensity, tension, fear, and anger all fuel strong wanting.

- ❧ Release any fixation on a certain outcome. Recognize that all you can do is tend to the causes, but you can't force the results (chapter 37).

- ❧ Keep the sense of "me" to a minimum. Success or failure will come from dozens of factors, only a few of which are under your control. Win or lose, don't take it personally.

Along the way, watch out for the widespread belief that if you're not fiercely driven toward your goals, you're kind of a wimp. Remember that you can have strong effort toward your aims without falling into attachment to the results. Consider the description I once heard of Thich Nhat Hanh, a Vietnamese monk who has accomplished many things as a peace advocate and teacher:

A cloud, a butterfly, and a bulldozer

31
Keep Going

I once attended a workshop led by Joseph Goldstein, a Buddhist teacher. I had realized something about the lack of a fixed self, and shared the insight with him. He nodded and said, "Yes, right." I felt seen for taking a step forward. Then he smiled and added something I've never forgotten: "Keep going."

Of all the factors that lead to happiness and success—such as class origins, intelligence, personality, character, looks, luck, race,—the one that typically makes the most difference over time is *persistence*. Knocked down ten times, you get up ten times.

If you keep going, you *might* not reach your goal—but if you stop, you'll *never* reach it.

We respect people who persist. There's a magic in determination that draws others toward it and elicits their support.

And you just don't know when your day will finally come. There are so many stories of "overnight success" that actually arrived after many years of effort, often including some failures. For example, Dwight Eisenhower was an obscure colonel in 1939—and nearly forty-nine years old—when Germany invaded Poland to begin World War II; four years later he was in charge of all Allied forces in Europe; nine years after that he was elected president.

How

Make sure your goals are worthy of your perseverance. You can be determined to a fault. Don't "keep going" down a tunnel with no cheese. Consider the collateral damage: are you winning battles but losing the "war" of overall health, well-being, integrity, and welfare of others?

Know the feeling of tenacious persistence. It could be fierce, strong, stubborn, unyielding, clear, inspired, surrendered, on-mission, purposeful, focused, committed—or all of these. Recall a time you had this feeling, and know it again in your body. Call it up whenever you need to draw on resources inside to keep going.

Take the step that's right in front of you—one after another. I've taught many people to rock climb: Beginners will often have one foot down low and one foot at knee level, on solid placements, plus two good handholds, yet they can't find any new holds, so they feel stuck. But when they simply stand up on the higher foothold—taking the step that's available—that brings higher handholds and footholds within reach.

Find the pace you can sustain; life's a marathon, not a sprint. For example, on my first Boy Scout backpack trip, I was a skinny, nerdy, unathletic kid. But I wanted to be the first to our campsite. We set out and the burly "alpha" boys raced ahead, while I kept up a slow-but-steady pace. After a few miles, I passed them sitting down on the side of the trail. They were startled to see me trucking along and soon got up and raced past me. But after another few miles, once again they were laid out by the side of the trail, this time really fried as I walked past them—and I was very happy to get the first, really cool tent spot.

Keep going in your mind even if you can't make any headway in the world. Maybe you're truly stuck in some situation—a job, an illness, a certain sort of marriage. But at least you can continue to reflect on what's happening, learn to cope with it better, and love the people around you. And over time maybe things will improve. As Winston Churchill said, "If you're going through hell, keep going."

Have faith that your efforts will pay off. You may have heard this teaching story: A bunch of frogs fell into a vat of cream. They couldn't jump out, and one after another drowned. But one frog refused to quit and kept swimming and staying alive, even after all the other frogs had died. Finally its movements churned the cream to solid butter—and it hopped out to safety.

Keep churning!

part four:

Engage the World

32

Be Curious

A couple years ago, my father and I were driving to the ocean, near where I live north of San Francisco. Born on a ranch in North Dakota in 1918, he's a retired zoologist who loves birds, and I wanted to show him some wetlands.

The twisting road was carved from the side of coastal hills plunging to the sea. After a while we paused at a pull-out for a pit stop. Returning from the bushes, I found my dad scrutinizing dried, scraggly grasses sticking out from the mini-cliff next to our car. "Look, Rick," he said excitedly, "see how the layers of dirt are different, so the plants growing in them are different, too!" He sounded like a little kid who'd discovered an elephant in his backyard.

But that's my dad: endlessly curious, never bored. I and ten thousand other drivers had sped around that turn seeing nothing but another meaningless road cut. But he had not taken the commonplace for granted. He wondered about what he saw and looked for connections, explanations. For him, the world wears a question mark.

This attitude of wonder, interest, and investigation brings many rewards. For example, engaging your mind actively as you age helps preserve the functioning of your brain. Use it or lose it!

Plus you gather lots of useful information—about yourself, other people, the world—by looking around. You also see the larger context, and thus become less affected by any single thing itself: not so driven to get more of what you like, and not so stressed and unsettled by what you don't like.

As our daughter once pointed out, curious people are typically not self-centered. Sure, they are interested in the inner workings of their own psyche—curiosity is a great asset for healing, growth, and awakening—but they're also very engaged with the world and others. Maybe that's why we usually like curious people.

How

To begin with, curiosity requires a *willingness* to see whatever is under the rocks you turn over. Usually it's neutral or positive. But occasionally you find something that looks creepy or smells bad. Then you need courage, to face an uncomfortable aspect of yourself, other people, or the world. In this case, it helps to observe it from a distance, and try not to identify with it. Surround it with spaciousness, knowing that whatever you've found is just one part of a larger whole and (usually) a passing phenomenon.

With that willingness, curiosity expresses itself in action, through looking deeper and wider—and then looking again.

Much of what we're curious about is really neat, such as the development of children, the doings of friends, or the workings of a new computer. And sometimes it pays to be curious about some sort of issue. As an illustration, let's say you've been feeling irritable about a situation. (You also can apply the practices below to different aspects of your mind, or to other people or to situations in the world.)

Looking deeper means being interested in what's under the surface. For example, what previous situations does it remind you of—particularly ones when you were young and most affected by things?

Looking wider means broadening your view:

- What are other aspects of the situation, such as the good intentions of others, or your own responsibility for events?

- What factors could be at work in your mind? For example, have you worked too much lately, or felt underappreciated, or not eaten or slept well? Did you appraise the situation as a lot worse, or a lot more threatening, than it actually was? Did you take it personally?

Looking again means being active in your investigating. You keep unraveling the knot of whatever you're curious about, teasing apart the threads, opening them up and seeing what's what. You don't take the first explanation as the final one. There's an underlying attitude of wonder and fearlessness. Like a child, a cat, a scientist, a saint, or a poet, you see the world anew.

Again.

And again.

33
Enjoy Your Hands

Sometimes it's worth remembering the obvious: you engage the world with your *body*—often with your *hands*.

Human hands are unique in the animal kingdom in their dexterity and sensitivity. Their capacity for skilled action helped drive the evolution of the neural networks that handle sophisticated planning, decision-making, and self-control.

Your hands reach, touch, caress, hold, manipulate, and let go. They type, stir pots, brush hair, wash dishes, shift gears, scratch ears, open doors, throw stones, hold loved ones, and help you snuggle into bed. They may not be perfect, and with aging, they may sometimes be in pain, but they're always lovely and vital.

Appreciating your hands makes you appreciate living. Being mindful of them—paying attention to what they're feeling and doing—is a simple and available way to drop down into a more sensual, in-the-body connection with the world, including the people you touch.

How

Right now, take a moment to be aware of your hands. What are they doing? What are they touching? They are always touching something, if only the air. What are they sensing? Warm or cool? Hard or soft?

Move your fingertips. Notice how incredibly sensitive they are, with about 20,000 nerve endings per square inch. Play with the sensations of your fingers stroking your palm, your thumb touching each finger in turn, the fingers of one hand caressing the fingers of the other one.

Soak up the enjoyment your hands give you. Use your hands to draw you into pleasure such as the warmth of holding a cup of coffee, the relief of scratching an itchy head, or the satisfaction of getting a pesky button through its hole.

As appropriate, touch others more. Feel the grip of a handshake, a friend's shoulder, a lover's skin, a child's hair, a dog's or cat's fur.

Feel the skillfulness of your hands: steering a car, writing a note, replacing a lightbulb, sawing wood, planting bulbs, measuring garlic, peeling an onion. Feel their strength in holding a knife, making a fist, lugging a suitcase.

Watch your hands talk: pointing, rising and falling, opening and closing, thumbs-up, okay, waving hello and goodbye.

Many times a day, try to sink awareness into your hands.

Feel them feeling your life.

34
Don't Know

Once upon a time, a scholar and a saint lived on the same street, and they arranged to meet. The scholar asked the saint about the meaning of life. She said a few words about love and joy, then paused to reflect, and the scholar jumped in with a long discourse on Western and Eastern philosophy. When the scholar was finished, the saint proposed some tea, prepared it with care, and began pouring it slowly into the scholar's cup. Inch by inch the tea rose. It approached the lip of the cup, and she kept pouring. It ran over the top of the cup and onto the table, and she still kept pouring. The scholar burst out: "What are you doing?! You can't put more into a cup that's already full!" The saint set down the teapot and said, "Exactly."

A mind that's open and spacious can absorb lots of useful information. On the other hand, a mind that's already full—of assumptions, beliefs about the intentions of others, preconceived ideas—misses important details or contexts, jumps to conclusions, and has a hard time learning anything new.

For example, let's say a friend says something hurtful to you. What benefits would come from an initial attitude that's something like this: *Hmm, what's this about? I'm not sure, don't entirely know.* First, you'd buy yourself time to figure things out before putting your foot in your mouth. Second, you'd naturally investigate and learn more: Did you hear correctly? Did you do something wrong you should apologize for? Is something bothering your friend unrelated to you? Did your friend simply misunderstand you? Third, she'd probably be more open and less defensive with you; a know-it-all is pretty irritating.

The great child psychologist Jean Piaget proposed that there are essentially two kinds of learning:

- *Assimilation*—We incorporate new information into an existing belief system.
- *Accommodation*—We change a belief system based on new information.

Both are important, but accommodation is more fundamental and far-reaching. Nonetheless, it's harder to do, since abandoning or transforming long-held beliefs can feel dizzying, even frightening. That's why it's important to keep finding our way back to that wonderful openness a child has, seeing a cricket or toothbrush or mushroom for the very first time: child mind, beginner's mind . . . don't-know mind.

How

For a few minutes, or for a day, a week—or a lifetime—let yourself not know:

- Be especially skeptical of what you're sure is true. These are the beliefs that often get us in the most trouble.

- In conversation, don't assume you know where other people are headed. Don't worry about what you're going to say; you'll figure it out just fine when it's your turn. Remember how you feel when someone acts like they know what you're "really" thinking, feeling, or wanting.

- Let your eyes travel over familiar objects—like the stuff on a dinner table—and notice what it's like during that brief interval, maybe a second or so, after you've focused on an object but before the verbal label (e.g., "salt," "glass") has come into awareness.

- Or go for a walk. Notice how the mind tries to categorize and label—to know—the things around you, so it can solve problems and keep you alive. Appreciate your mind—"Good boy! Good girl!"—and then explore letting go of needing to know.

- Ask yourself if it's important to you to be a person with the right answers, the one who knows. What would it be like to lay down that burden?

⋇ This may seem a little cosmic, but it's down-to-earth: Look at something and ask yourself if you know what it *is*. Suppose it's a cup. Do you really know what a "cup" is, deep down? You say it's made of atoms, of electrons, protons, quarks. But do you know what a quark is? You say it's energy, or space-time, or sparkling fairy dust beyond human ken, or whatever—but really, do you ever, can you ever, actually know what energy or space-time truly is?? We live our lives surrounded by objects that we navigate and manipulate—spoons, cars, skyscrapers—while never truly knowing what any of it actually *is*. And neither does anyone else, even the world's greatest scientists.

⋇ Since you don't really know what a spoon is, do you even know what you are? Or what you are truly capable of? Or how high you could actually soar? Consider any limiting assumptions about your own life . . . how you've "known" that your ideas were not very good, that others would laugh (or that it would matter if they did), that no one would back you, that swinging for the fences just means striking out. What happens if you apply "don't know" to these assumptions?

⋇ Notice how relaxing and good it feels to lighten up about needing to know. Take in those good feelings so you'll feel more comfortable hanging out in don't-know mind.

May you know less after this practice of not-knowing than when you began.

And therefore, know more than ever!

35
Do What You Can

Researchers have shown that it is remarkably easy to produce "learned helplessness" in dogs, whose neural circuitry for motivation and emotion is quite similar to ours. Then it takes much, much more training to get the dogs to unlearn their helpless passivity (Seligman 1972).

People are much the same. We, too, can be easily trained in learned helplessness, which can be tough to undo. Think about some of the ways you've felt pushed around by external forces, and how that's affected you. Learned helplessness fosters depression, anxiety, pessimism, low self-worth, and less effort toward goals.

As a human being like any other, your biological vulnerability to learned helplessness makes it very important that you *recognize* where you do in fact have some power, and that you take the actions that *are* available to you—even if they must be only inside your own head.

How

Begin by considering a useful idea from Stephen Covey's book *The Seven Habits of Highly Effective People*. Imagine a circle containing the things you have influence over, and another circle containing the things you're concerned about. Where those circles overlap is the sweet spot where you can actually make a difference in the things that matter to you.

To be sure, sometimes there are things we care about but can't change personally, like people going hungry. I'm not saying just ignore those things or be indifferent to them. We should focus on what we *can* do, such as bearing witness to the suffering of others and letting it move our hearts, staying informed, and looking for opportunities to make a material difference, such as helping at a homeless shelter.

But trying to control things that are out of your hands will plant seeds of helplessness, make you suffer, and undermine your capacity to exercise the influence you do have.

Ask yourself: How could I pull my time, money, energy, attention, or worry away from stones that will never give blood or houses built on sand—and instead, shift these resources to where they will *actually* make a difference?

Then take an inventory of the key strengths and other resources you *do* have. Your circle of influence is probably a lot bigger than you think it is!

Consider how you could draw on some of those resources to take beneficial actions in ways you haven't ever done, or have never sustained. Challenge assumptions, like: "Oh, I just couldn't do *that*." Are you sure? Bring to mind someone you know who is very self-confident, and then ask yourself: "If I were that confident, what new things would I do?"

In particular, think about actions you could take inside your own mind. Compared to trying to change the world or your body, usually your mind is where you have the most influence, where the results are most enduring and consequential, and where you have the greatest opportunity for a sense of efficacy and a chance to undo feelings of helplessness. For example, how could you nudge your emotional reactions in a better direction over time, or develop more mindfulness or warm-heartedness? These are all within your reach.

When I don't know what to do about some difficulty, sometimes I think of a saying from a boy named Nkosi Johnson, who lived in South Africa. Like many children there, Nkosi was born with HIV, and he died when he was twelve. Before that happened, he became a nationally known advocate for people with AIDS. His "mantra," as he called it, always touches my heart: "Do all you can, with what you have, in the time you have, in the place where you are."

That's all anyone can ever do.

36

Accept the Limits
of Your Influence

The previous practice was to exercise the influence you *do* have: to do what you can.

Of course, it's also true that each one of us is very limited in what we can do or change. You can't change the past, or even this present moment. Looking to the future—the only thing you can actually affect—you have little influence over other people, including their thoughts, actions, or suffering. And even less influence over the economy, government policies, or international affairs. Things happen due to causes—and of the ten thousand causes upstream of this moment, most of them are out of your control.

You don't have the power to make something happen if the prerequisites aren't present. For example, you can't grow roses without good soil and water.

If you've been pounding your head against a wall for a while, it's time to stop, accept the way it is, and move on. As I sometimes tell myself: *Don't try to grow roses in a parking lot.*

How

In general, when faced with some fact you can't change—like you're stuck in traffic, or you feel sad, or your young daughter has just poured milk on the floor (speaking of some of my own experiences)—ask yourself, *Can I accept that this is the way it is, whether I like it or not?*

Understand that acceptance does *not* mean approval, acquiescence, overlooking, or forgiveness. You are simply facing the facts, including the fact of your limited influence.

Notice the good feelings that come with acceptance, even if there are also painful feelings about various facts. Notice that acceptance usually brings you more resources for dealing with life's difficulties.

If you cannot accept a fact—that it exists, that it has happened, whatever your preferences may be—then see if you can accept the fact that you cannot accept the fact!

More specifically, consider these reflections:

- Review a life event that has troubled you. See if you can accept it as something that happened, like it or not—and as truly just a part of a much larger and probably mainly positive whole.

❧ Consider an aspect of your body or personality that you don't like. Tell the truth to yourself about the extent to which you can change it and make a clear choice as to what you will actually do. Then see if you can accept whatever remains as just the way it is—and as only a small part of the much larger and generally positive whole that is you.

❧ Bring to mind a key person in your life. Have there been any ways that you've been trying to affect or change this person that are just not working? What limits to your influence here do you need to accept?

❧ Consider something you've wanted to happen but been frustrated about—perhaps a career shift, or a certain school working out for your child, or a sale to a new customer. Are the necessary supporting conditions truly present? If they are, then maybe stick with it and be patient. But if they are not present—if you're trying to grow roses in a parking lot—consider shifting your hopes and efforts in another direction.

37

Tend to the Causes

Let's say you want to have your own apple tree. So you go to a nursery and pick out a good sapling, bring it home, and plant it carefully with lots of fertilizer in rich soil. Then you water it regularly, pick the bugs off, and prune it. If you keep tending to your tree, in a few years it will likely give you lots of delicious apples.

But can you *make* it grow apples? Nope, you can't. All you can do is tend to the causes—but you can't control the results. No one can. The most powerful person in the world can't make a tree produce an apple.

Similarly, a teacher cannot make his students learn long division, a business owner can't make her employees invent new products, and you cannot make someone love you. All we can do is promote the causes of the results we want.

This truth has two implications, one tough-minded and another that's peaceful:

❧ You are responsible for the causes you *can* tend to. If you are not getting the results you want in your life, ask yourself: Am I truly doing everything I reasonably can to promote the causes of those results?

❧ You can relax attachment to results. When you understand that much of what determines whether they happen or not is out of your hands, you worry less about whether they'll happen, and you suffer less if they don't.

Paradoxically, focusing less on results and more on causes improves the odds of getting the results you want: you zero in on creating the factors that lead to success, and you aren't worn down by stressing over the outcome.

How

❧ Do what you can to lift your personal well-being. This is a *global* factor that will turbocharge all the other causes you tend to.

So ask yourself: what makes the most difference to my well-being? It could be something that seems little; for me, a big factor is when I go to bed, since that determines whether I can wake up in time to meditate in the morning, which transforms my whole day. It could also mean dropping something that brings you down, like needless arguments with other people.

Pick *one* thing that will lift your well-being and focus on this for a while.

❧ Also consider a key area in your life where you are not getting the results you want, such as work, love, health, fun, or spirituality. In that area, identify one cause that will have big effects. For example, in a logjam, there's usually a "key log" that will free up the whole mess if you get *it* to move.

For example, if you want to lose weight, tend to the cause of exercise. If you want a mate, tend to the cause of meeting new "qualified prospects." If you want your kids to cooperate, tend to the cause of parental authority. If you want a better job, tend to the cause of an organized job search. If you want more peace of mind, tend to the cause of routinely relaxing your body.

❧ Tell the truth to yourself about causes and results: Are you pursuing the right causes of the results you're seeking? Or are you pulling hard on a rope (a cause) that's just not attached to the load you're trying to move (the result you want)?

Maybe you need to tend to other causes— perhaps ones at a deeper level, such as letting go of self-doubt or fear from childhood. Or perhaps the result you want is out of your power, and you just have to accept that.

Let the results be what they are, learn from them, and then turn your attention back to causes. Don't get so caught up in your apples that you forget to water their tree!

38

Don't Be Alarmed

The nervous system has been evolving for about 600 million years. During all this time, creatures—worms, crabs, lizards, rats, monkeys, hominids, humans—that were real mellow, watching the sunlight on the leaves, getting all Zen, absorbed in inner peace . . . CHOMP got eaten because they didn't notice the shadow overhead or crackle of twigs nearby.

The ones that survived to pass on their genes were fearful and vigilant—and we are their great-great-grand-children, bred to be afraid. Even though we've come a long way from the Serengeti, we're still quick to feel unsettled in any situation that seems the least bit threatening: not enough time to get through your e-mails, more news of a struggling economy, no call after two days from someone you've started dating, and so on.

Even if the situations you're in are reasonably good, there are other, innate sources of alarm rooted in our biology. Basically, to survive, animals—including us— must continually try to:

- ◄ Separate themselves from the world
- ◄ Stabilize many dynamic systems in the body, mind, relationships, and environment
- ◄ Get rewards and avoid harms

But here's the problem: each of these strategies flies in the face of the facts of existence:

- ◄ Everything is connected to everything else—so it's impossible to fundamentally separate self and world.
- ◄ Everything changes—so it's impossible to keep things stable in the body, mind, relationships, or environment.
- ◄ Rewards are fleeting, costly, or unobtainable, and some harms are inevitable—so it's impossible to hold onto pleasure forever and totally escape pain.

Alarms sound whenever one of these strategies runs into trouble—which is many times a day because of the contradictions between the nature of existence and what we must do to survive. Alarms below awareness create a background of unease, irritability, caution, and pessimism; the ones you're consciously aware of are emotionally and often physically uncomfortable—such as anxiety, anger, or pain.

157

Don't underestimate the amount of background alarm in your body and mind. It's hard-wired and relentless, inherent in the collision between the needs of life and the realities of existence.

While this alarmism has been a great strategy for keeping creatures alive to pass on their genes, it's not good for your health, well-being, relationships, or ambitions. Threat signals are usually way out of proportion to what is actually happening. They make you pull in your wings and play safe and small, and cling tighter to "us" and fear "them." At the level of groups and nations, our vulnerability to alarm makes us easy to manipulate with fear.

Yes, deal with real threats, real harms—but enough with all these false alarms!

How

Take a stand for yourself: "I'm tired of being needlessly afraid." Consider the price you've paid over the years due to false alarms: the running for cover, the muzzling of self-expression, the abandonment of important longings or aspirations.

Try to be more aware of the subtle sense of alarm, such as a tightening in your chest or face, a sinking feeling in your stomach, a sense of being off balance, or an increase in scanning or guardedness.

Then recognize that many alarm signals are actually not signals at all: they're just unpleasant *noise*, meaningless, like a car alarm that won't stop blapping. Obviously, deal with real alarms. But as for the ones that are exaggerated or entirely bogus, don't react to these alarms with alarm.

Accept that bad things sometimes happen, there are uncertainties, planes do occasionally crash, nice people get hit by drunk drivers. We just have to live with the fact that we can't dodge all the bullets. When you come to peace with this, you stop trying to control—out of alarm—the things you can't.

Keep helping your body feel less alarmed. I imagine my "inner iguana" lodged in the most ancient and fearful structures of the brainstem, and gently stroking its belly, soothing and settling it so it relaxes like a lizard on a warm rock. The same with my inner rat, or monkey, or caveman: continually softening and opening the body, breathing fully and letting go, sensing strength and resolve inside.

Alarms may clang, but your awareness and intentions are much larger—like the sky dwarfing clouds. In effect, alarms and fears are held in a space of fearlessness. You see this zig-zaggy, up-and-down world clearly—and you are at peace with it. Try to return to this open-hearted fearlessness again and again throughout your day.

39
Put Out Fires

In your heart, right now, you know if there are any vital matters that you're not dealing with: a harm or threat that's not being addressed, or a major lost opportunity. These are real alarms, and you need to listen to them.

For example, there could be unpaid bills on the verge of harming your credit score, a teenager who's increasingly disrespectful and defiant—or caught in the undertow of depressed mood—month after month without much exercise, a marriage that's unraveling thread by thread, abuse of alcohol or drugs, a co-worker who keeps undermining you, chronic overeating, or a nagging sense that there's something wrong with your health.

Quickly or slowly, "fires" like these will singe a life, and sometimes burn it to the ground.

If something's urgent—such as a clogged toilet, a letter from the IRS, a lump in an armpit—most people will get after it right away. But what if it's important-but-not-urgent—an issue or goal that you can always put off dealing with for one more day? It's easy to let these fires smolder—but in the end, they're the ones that usually cost you the most. You still know they're out there; they cast a shadow you can feel in your gut. And eventually their consequences always come home—sometimes during your last years, when you look back on your life and consider what you wish you'd done differently.

On the other hand, when you come to grips with important things, even if they're not urgent, that unease in the belly goes away. You feel good about yourself, doing what you can and making your life better.

How

Open to an intuition, a sense, of whatever you may have pushed to the back burner that truly needs attending. Consider your health, finances, relationships, well-being, and (if this is meaningful to you) spiritual life. Notice any reluctance to face significant unmet needs—it's normal to feel guilty or anxious about them—and see if you can release it.

Ask yourself: what gets in the way of you addressing important-but-not-urgent matters in a typical day? What do you finesse or manage each day but never solve once and for all? Or what do you keep postponing altogether?

What's not actually getting better no matter how much you hope it will?

Write down the name(s) of the important thing(s) you need to address. Tell a trusted person about this. Make it real for yourself that this issue *matters*. Face it. Keep facing it.

Bring to mind some of the many benefits that will come to you and others if you tackle this issue. Help them be vivid in your mind. See how your days will improve, how you'll sleep better, feel better, and love better. Open to your heart's longing for these benefits. Let the benefits call you, drawing you like honey does a bee.

Also bring to mind the short- and long-term costs to you and others of this issue continuing to smolder away. Be honest with yourself—willing to feel guilt, remorse, or shame in order to do the so honorable, so hard thing of looking squarely at these costs.

Feeling the benefits, and feeling the costs, make a choice: Are you going to put out this fire? Or wait another day?

When you choose to confront this issue, open to feeling good about that.

Then get to work. You don't need to have a complete plan to get started. Just know the first step or two—such as talking about the issue with a friend or therapist, gathering information (e.g., assessing a health concern), seeing a professional, doing one or more small positive actions each day, or getting structured support from others (e.g., a buddy to exercise with, a regular AA meeting). If you're stuck, you don't need a more perfect plan; you need to take imperfect action. The breakthrough will come when you *commit* to addressing an issue and then *structure* ongoing support and action toward that end.

If you find yourself procrastinating or getting bogged down, imagine that you are looking back on your life as you near its end. From that perspective, what will you be glad that you did?

40
Dream Big Dreams

Everyone has dreams: goals, big plans, reasons for living, contributions to others. They include starting a family, changing careers, going to college, deepening the emotionally and sensually intimate aspects of a long-term relationship, writing a book, living a spiritual practice, making art, getting a stoplight installed at a dangerous intersection, losing thirty pounds and keeping it off, saving the whales, saving the world.

Many of these dreams are rooted in childhood visions of what's possible. When the young elements are peeled away, what remains is often still deeply true for a person.

What are your own longings of the heart?

They could be quite concrete—and still be big dreams. Like everybody in the family doing their share of housework. Or finding a job that takes less than an hour to drive to. Or coming to peace with your mother or your son. Or planting roses. Or carving out half an hour a day for yourself.

Or they could be more far-reaching or lofty. Such as reducing bullying in schools or carbon dumping in the atmosphere, or pursuing your own spiritual awakening.

If you truly open to this question—*What are the dreams that matter to me?*—don't worry, you won't get caught up in silly stuff, such as wanting to get super rich and famous. Instead, you'll hear your soul speaking—your essence, your core, your deepest inner wisdom.

It's worth listening to what it says.

And then worth looking for ways—practical ones, grounded in daily life, that move you forward one real step at a time—to bring your dreams to life.

How

Find a quiet time and place, and ask yourself what you long for. Also imagine younger versions of yourself, and ask them what their dreams are.

Try to be open to what comes up, rather than dismissing it as unrealistic, too late, "selfish," or foolish. Perhaps write it down, even just a few words, or tell someone. If you like, make a collage of pictures (and maybe words) that represent your dream(s). And remember that your dreams aren't set in stone; you can let them breathe and change and grow.

Make room for your dreams in your thoughts and actions. Be their friend. Feel what it would be like if they came true, and how that would be good for you and others.

Without getting bogged down in details or obstructions, give thought to what you could do, in realistic ways, to move toward the fulfillment of your dreams. Look for the small things you can implement and build on each day. Perhaps go further and write down a plan for yourself, with—gulp—dates on it. Don't be daunted by things getting more real.

Then take action. If it helps, tell the truth about and keep a record of your actions—like writing down how much time you spend each day exercising, talking lovingly with your mate, or simply curled up relaxing. Focus on the things that will make the most difference; put the big rocks in the bucket first.

Throughout, let your dream live *you*. Feel into the wholesome heart of a dream—how it comes from deep within, how it is healthy, how it will serve you and others. Give yourself over to your dream.

Let your dream be a friend to you.

41

Be Generous

Giving—to others, to the world, to oneself—is deep in our nature as human beings.

When our mammalian ancestors first appeared, about two hundred million years ago, their capacities for bonding, emotion, and generosity were extraordinary evolutionary breakthroughs. Unlike reptiles and fish, mammals and birds care for their young, pair bond (sometimes for life), and usually form complex social groups organized around various kinds of cooperation. This takes more smarts than, say, a fish laying a swarm of eggs and swimming away—so in proportion to body weight, mammals and birds have bigger brains than reptiles and fish do.

When primates came along about sixty million years ago, there was another jump in brain size based on the "reproductive advantages" (love that phrase) of social abilities. The primate species that are the most relational—that have the most complex communications, grooming, alpha/

beta hierarchies, and so on—have the largest cortex (in proportion to weight).

Then early hominids emerged, starting to make stone tools about 2.5 million years ago. Since then, the brain has tripled in size, and much of this new cortex is devoted to interpersonal skills such as language, empathy, attachment to family and friends, romance, cooperative planning, and altruism. As the brain enlarged, a longer childhood was required to allow for its growth after birth and to make good use of its wonderful new capabilities. This necessitated more help from fathers to keep children and their mothers alive during the uniquely long juvenile phase of a human life, and more help from "the village it takes to raise a child." The bonding and nurturing of primate mothers— in a word, their *giving*—gradually evolved into romantic love, fathers caring for their young, friendship, and the larger web of affiliations that join humans together. Additionally, our ancestors bred mainly within their own band; bands that were better at the give-and-take of relationships and teamwork out-competed other bands for scarce resources, so the genes that built more socially intelligent brains proliferated into the human genome. In sum, giving, broadly defined, both enabled and drove the evolution of the brain over millions of years.

Consequently, we swim in a sea of generosity—of many daily acts of consideration, reciprocity, benevolence, compassion, kindness, helpfulness, warmth, appreciation, respect, patience, forbearance, and contribution—but like those proverbial fish, often don't realize we're wet. Because of the brain's negativity bias, moments of not-giving—one's own resentments and selfishness, and the withholding and unkindness of others—pop out with blazing headlines. Plus modern economies can make it seem like giving and getting is largely about making money—but that part of life is just a tiny fraction of the original and still vast "generosity economy," with its circular flows of freely given, unmonetized goods and services.

When you express your giving nature, it feels good for you, benefits others, prompts them to be good to you in turn, and adds one more lovely thread to the great tapestry of human generosity.

How

Take care of yourself. Don't give in ways that harm you or others (e.g., offering a blind eye to someone's alcoholism). Keep refueling yourself; it's easier to give when your own cup runneth over—or at least you're not running on empty.

Prime the pump of generosity. Be aware of things you are grateful for or glad about. Bring to mind a sense of already being full, so that you'll not feel deprived or emptied out if you give a little more.

Notice that giving is natural for you. You don't need to be a saint to be a giving person. Generosity comes in many forms, including heart, time, self-control, service, food, and money. From this perspective, consider how much you already give each day. Open to feeling good about yourself as a giver.

Give your full attention. Stay present with others minute after minute, staying with their topic or agenda. You may not like what they say, but you could still offer a receptive ear. (Especially important with a child or mate.) Then, when it's your turn, the other person will likely feel better about you taking the microphone.

Offer nonreactivity. Much of the time, interactions, relationships, and life altogether would go better if we did not add our comments, advice, or emotional reactions to a situation. Not-doing is sometimes the best gift.

Be helpful. For example, volunteer for a school, give money to a good cause, or increase your own housework or child care if your partner is doing more than you.

Do your own practice. One of your best contributions to others is to raise your own level of well-being and functioning. Whatever your practice is or could grow to be, do it with a whole heart, as a daily offering to whatever you hold sacred, to your family and friends, and to the widening world.

part five:

Be at Peace

42

Notice You're All Right Right Now

To keep our ancestors alive, the brain evolved an ongoing internal trickle of unease. This little whisper of worry keeps you scanning your inner and outer worlds for signs of trouble.

This background of unsettledness and watchfulness is so automatic that you can forget it's there. So see if you can tune in to a tension, guarding, or bracing in your body. Or a vigilance about your environment or other people. Or a block against *completely* relaxing, letting down, letting go. Try to walk through an office or store that you know is safe without a molecule of wariness: it's really hard. Or try to sit at home for five minutes straight while feeling undefended, soft in your body, utterly comfortable in the moment as it is, at peace: this is impossible for most people.

The brain's default setting of apprehensiveness is a great way to keep a monkey looking over its shoulder for something about to pounce. But it's a crummy way to live. It wears down well-being, feeds anxiety and depression, and makes people play small in life.

And it's based on a lie.

In effect, that uneasiness in the background is continually whispering in your mental "ear": You're not safe, you're surrounded by threats, you can never afford to lower your guard.

But take a close look at *this* moment, right now. Probably, you are basically all right: no one is attacking you, you are not drowning, no bombs are falling, there is no crisis. It's not perfect, but you're okay.

By "right now," I mean *this* moment. When we go into the future, we worry and plan. When we go into the past, we resent and regret. Threads of fear are woven into the mental tapestries of past and future. Look again at the thin slice of time that is the *present*. In this moment: Are you basically okay? Is breathing okay? Is the heart beating? Is the mind working? The answers are almost certainly yes.

In daily life, it's possible to access this fundamental sense of all-rightness even while getting things done. You're not ignoring real threats or issues, or pretending that everything is perfect. It's not. But in the middle of everything, you can usually see that you're actually all right right now.

How?

Several times a day, notice that you're basically all right.

You may want more money or love, or simply ketchup for your French fries. Or want less pain, heartache, or rush hour traffic. All very reasonable. But meanwhile, underneath all the to-ing and fro-ing, you are okay. Underneath your desires and activities is an aliveness and an awareness that is doing fine this second.

There you are fixing dinner; notice that *"I'm all right right now,"* and perhaps say that softly in your mind. Or you're driving: *I'm all right right now.* Or you're talking with someone: *I'm all right right now.* Or doing e-mails or putting a child to bed: *I'm all right right now.*

Notice that, while feeling all right right now, you can still get things done and deal with problems. The fear that bad things will happen if you let yourself feel okay is unfounded; let this sink in. You do not need to fear feeling all right!

Sometimes you're really *not* all right. Maybe something terrible has happened, or your body is very disturbed, or your mind is very upset. Do what you can at these times to ride out the storm. But as soon as possible, notice that the core of your being is okay, like the quiet place fifty feet underwater, beneath a hurricane howling above the sea.

Noticing that you're actually all right right now is not laying a positive attitude over your life like a pretty veil. Instead, you are knowing a simple but profound fact: *In this moment I am all right*. You are sensing the truth in your body, deeper than fear, that it is breathing and living

174

and okay. You are recognizing that your mind is functioning fine no matter how nutty and not-fine the contents swirling through it are.

Settling into this basic sense of okayness is a powerful way to build well-being and resources in your brain and being. You're taking a stand for the truth—and against the lies murmured by Mother Nature.

43
Honor Your Temperament

As hominids and early humans evolved over several million years while living in small bands, they developed a range of temperaments, with cautious, focused "turtles" at one end and adventurous, impulsive "jackrabbits" at the other end, with "tweeners" in the middle. Those bands that had a mixture of turtles, tweeners, and jackrabbits could adapt to changing conditions and outcompete bands that had just one type of temperament—the way a basketball team with nimble guards plus big forwards would beat teams with only guards or only forwards.

For similar reasons, we also evolved diversity in other aspects of temperament, including:

- Sociability—Some people are really extroverted, some are really introverted, and many are in the middle. In a general sense, with lots of exceptions in the details, extroverts are fed by social contact and drained by isolation; introverts are the opposite.

◄ Emotional inclinations—The ancient Greek model of the four personality types—sanguine (cheerful), choleric (prone to irritation), melancholic (tends to sadness), and phlegmatic (hard to move emotionally)—has at least a grain of truth to it.

Temperamental characteristics are innate, hard-wired into your DNA and thus your brain. Of course, they're just some of the tiles that make up the mosaic you are. Plus they're only *tendencies* whose expression is shaped by other parts of you (e.g., intelligence, warmheartedness), life experiences, and conscious intention. For example, I'm introverted but also love deep conversations (a typical therapist); so after a day of being with people, I get refueled by some time alone: reading, going for a run, and the like. Similarly, a person with a bit of a blue streak (i.e., melancholic) can internalize a soothing, encouraging sense of being cared about by others. Temperament is not destiny.

Different temperaments are a good fit with certain environments (e.g., situations, tasks, people) and not such a good fit with other ones. For instance, a sensitive infant would do well with an easygoing parent who is well-supported by his or her partner, but not so well with a single parent who is worn out and irritable; a jackrabbity first-grader will usually flourish in an experiential learning setting that's like a big pasture with firm fences, but will likely get many little corrections—which are stressful and

177

dispiriting—in a classroom that's tightly controlled with lots of fine-motor table work; in a couple, things will go better if they find ways to give an introvert (like me) enough "cave" time and an extrovert (like my wife) enough connection, but worse if they don't.

When the fit between your temperament and an environment is not good, it's hard to function at your best—whether it was in school as a kid, or in an intimate relationship or at work today. Additionally, it's natural to feel at some level that there must be something wrong/weak/dumb/missing about you—which gets reinforced by any messages from the environment that, yep, the problem is with *you*, not it.

For example, a high degree of jackrabbititis now has its very own diagnosis—attention deficit/hyperactivity disorder (ADHD)—even though being jackrabbity has been wonderfully adaptive throughout most of the time humans and our hominid ancestors have lived on this planet. Further, people who are naturally wistful get told to cheer up and stop being mopey, introverts get told to go out and meet people, and turtles get told to stop being such sissies and jump into the deep end of the pool. This repeated sense that there's something not-right, not-optimal about oneself gradually sinks in and wears on a person's confidence, mood, and sense of worth.

But really, there's nothing wrong at all! We should each *honor* our temperament: accept it, see the things that are great about it, look for situations and relationships that play to its strengths, and take care of it when it's challenged (e.g., help a turtlish child get ready for anxiety-provoking transitions). In other words, work with nature, not against it.

How

Get a clear sense of your temperament. For example, compared to others of your age and gender, are you relatively:

- Distractible, impulsive, and stimulation-seeking? Or highly focused, judicious, and cautious?

- Interested in lots of social contact? Or in just a few good friends and considerable alone time?

- Cheerful, melancholic, easily irritated, or placid?

(It's fine to be in the middle of the range for these characteristics; then that would be what your temperament is.)

Think back on your childhood: did your temperament and your environments collide with each other significantly, leading either to criticism of you or simply a frustration inside that you couldn't be more successful academically or socially? As you consider this question, be kind to yourself. Remember that in childhood, it's the job of parents and teachers—who have many more options than kids do—to adapt environments as much as is possible and reasonable to the temperament of the child. Then consider the fit between you as an adult and your environments.

What are the strengths of your temperament? For example, people who are quick to anger are often quick to see injustice; children who are anxious are usually very conscientious; introverts have rich inner lives. What inclinations in your nature have been longing for more expression? Then consider the sorts of environments—such as occupations, romantic partners, settings, or schedules—that would support and draw on the strengths of your temperament. What could you do that's appropriate and skillful to nudge your current environments to play more to your strengths—or to get yourself into more suitable environments?

What are the needs or vulnerabilities in your temperament? For example, a spirited person needs a good deal of stimulation or life starts feeling like a thin soup; an extrovert needs a job with lots of interaction; a melancholic person is susceptible to feeling let down. Consider how you could address your needs and protect your vulnerabilities. For instance, if you're somewhat anxious by nature (I'd put myself in that boat), it's especially important to do what you can to create structure, predictability, and trust in your home and work.

Throughout these reflections, know that any issues have probably not been located in you or in your environments, but in the *fit* between you and them. Regarding yourself, have compassion for any stress or pain you may have experienced; appreciate the endurance and strength you've had in the times when you were the proverbial square peg in a round hole; challenge the expectations and other beliefs you've developed in collisions with your environments, such as a sense of inadequacy. Regarding your environments, consider them more as impersonal forces that may have been not good for you in some ways—while probably being suitable for at least some people—than as something inherently wrong or bad; consider if any forgiveness would be helpful to you here.

Last, appreciate the fact that no one has a perfect temperament. We're all pretty funky variations on the basic human model. Being able to see the humor in your temperament softens its edges and eases your interactions. For example, once as I was doing therapy, I squared my pad of paper to the edges of a small table. With a smile, my client teased me by reaching over to nudge the pad so it was now askew. We both laughed at my OCD-ish tendencies, which I'd disclosed in talking about her own. And then I squared the pad again because it bugged me so much!

44

Love Your Inner Child

As long as you've lived, your experiences have sifted down in your psyche, forming layers like the bands of colored rock in the Grand Canyon. The most fundamental layers were laid down in your childhood, when your brain was most impressionable.

Because of experience-dependent neuroplasticity, the things you felt, wanted, or believed as a child have been woven into your nervous system. For example, crying as an infant until someone came, joy at beginning to walk, fun with friends, feeling bad about yourself when scolded about schoolwork, power struggles with parents, wanting your body to be bigger/smaller/different in high school, wondering if anyone will like the real you, the bittersweet excitement of leaving home—whatever your own childhood was, experiences like these have sunk in to you and travel with you every day wherever you go.

Taken as a whole, these residues make up your inner child—which is not a silly cliché, but actually a large-scale system embedded in your brain that continually and powerfully influences your mood, sense of worth, expectations, and reactions. This child inside is at the core of who you are.

If you are embarrassed, ashamed, critical, controlling, squelching, pushy, or angry about this child, that will affect how you feel and how you act. Therefore, accepting the child parts within you, guiding them gently, and soaking your inner kid in cherishing nurturance will heal and feed the deepest layers of your psyche.

This inner child stuff can get conceptual, superficial, or merely sentimental. Instead, bring it down to the bone. Most childhoods are rocky, one way or another. As a kid, you probably felt hurt, were disappointed, felt like a loser, wanted recognition and love you didn't get, shelved some big dreams, and made decisions about yourself and life with the "logic" of a child. This is real. It had real effects. *And* you have a real chance today to be the strong, wise, and loving friend, coach, and yes, parent that you've always longed for.

How

Open to feeling cared *about* by someone. Next, move to feeling caring *toward* a friend, family member, or pet. Marinate in this sense of interest, support, and nurturance; let it fill your heart and mind. Then, staying grounded in the experience of caring, shift the target of this caring to *yourself*, especially yourself as a child.

Now, reflect back on your childhood as a whole, starting with your earliest memories. Stay with your *experience* of it, not the story line about it. What did it feel like to be a young child? To be in grade school? In high school? What were your happiest times? And most upsetting? What went well for you in your childhood—and badly? When did you feel really understood and supported—and not? What in you flourished in childhood—and what got bruised or wounded? What sort of kid were you—especially deep down? When did the best parts of you come out? What's become of them?

As much as you can, try to hold a sense of caring toward yourself while you engage these questions. Stay with your actual experience as a child, not critiquing it or justifying it, and definitely not shaming yourself for it. The vulnerable child inside everyone usually expects rejection, so it's afraid to show its teary, sniffly, snotty, whiny, needy, frightened, or angry face. Please don't push this child away. It wants to show itself but is afraid to. Make it safe for it to show itself to *you*.

Look for ways to bring the child inside you out to play. For example, my friend Leslie told me about moving to Wyoming and wandering in its extraordinary wilderness like a big kid, not trying to accomplish anything, feeling free and delighted. Take different routes to work; pick up (or return to) gardening, crafts, art, music, or a sport; quit being so darned serious and significant (this one's for me, too); goof off; play with your own kids; make messes; ask your inner child what he or she really wants to do. Don't be so constrained by routines and presumed limitations; remember what it felt like to be a kid on the first day of summer vacation; in the same way, the whole rest of your life stretches out before you: have fun with it!

Accept that you will never have a better childhood. Yes, assert yourself skillfully to get appropriate caring in your relationships. But also know the hard truth that it's on you, no one else, to be the main advocate, cheerleader, protector, and nurturer of the child inside—and the adult that kid has become. Keep both of them close to your heart.

45

Don't Throw Darts

Some physical and mental pain is inevitable. I remember being six and slipping on an icy sidewalk in Illinois and landing hard on my tailbone: ouch! Much later, in my fifties, when my mother passed away, there was a different kind of pain. To survive physically, you need a body that tells you it hurts when it's ill or injured. To flourish psychologically and in your relationships, you need a mind that sends different signals of distress—such as loneliness, anger, or fear—if you're rejected, mistreated, or threatened.

To use a metaphor from the Buddha, the unavoidable pains of life are its "first darts." But then we add insult to injury with our *reactions* to these darts. For example, you could react to a headache with anxiety that it might mean a brain tumor, or to being rejected in love with harsh self-criticism.

Further, it's common to have upsetting reactions when nothing bad has actually happened. For instance, you're flying in an airplane and everything's fine, but you're worried about it crashing. Or you go out on a date and it's fun, but then he/she doesn't call for a day and you feel let down.

Most absurdly, sometimes we react negatively to *positive* events. Perhaps someone complimented you, and you had feelings of unworthiness; or you've been offered an opportunity at work, and you obsess about whether you can handle it; or someone makes a bid for a deeper friendship, and you worry about being disappointing.

All these reactions are "second darts"—the ones we throw ourselves. They include overreacting to little things, holding grudges, justifying yourself, drowning in guilt after you've learned the lesson, dwelling on things long past, losing perspective, worrying about stuff you can't control, and mentally rehashing conversations.

Second darts vastly outnumber first darts. There you are, on the dartboard of life, bleeding mainly from self-inflicted wounds.

There are enough darts in life without adding your own!

How

Accept the inevitability of first darts. They hurt, but pain is the price of living. Try not to get offended by pain—as if it's an affront—or embarrassed about it, as if it's a personal failing.

When pain does come, hold it in a large space of awareness. In a traditional metaphor, imagine pouring a big spoon of salt into a cup of water and then drinking it: yuck. Next, imagine stirring that spoonful into a big bowl of clean water and drinking a cup: not so bad now. It's the same amount of salt—the same amount of physical or emotional pain—but now held and diluted in a larger context. Be aware of awareness: it's like the sky—pain passes through it like storm clouds, never tainting or harming awareness itself. See if you can let the pain be without reacting to it; this is a key aspect of an unconditional inner peace.

Observe second darts. They're often easier to see when others toss these darts at themselves—and then consider how you throw them at yourself. Gradually bring your recognition of second darts into the present moment, so you can see the inclination to throw them arise—and then catch them if possible before you stab yourself one more time.

A second dart will often trigger a cascade of mental reactions, like one boulder rolling down a mountainside setting off others in a chain reaction. To stop the landslide, start by relaxing your body as best you can. This will activate the calming, soothing parasympathetic wing of your nervous system and put the brakes on the fight-or-flight sympathetic wing.

Next, try to see more aspects of the situation that's troubled you, and more of your life these days altogether—especially the parts that are going fine. Because of the negativity bias, the brain narrows down and fixates on what's wrong, so you have to nudge it to widen its view to what's right. The bird's-eye, big picture view also deactivates the midline neural networks that do second-dart ruminating, and stimulates circuits on the side of your brain that can let things be as they are without reacting to them.

Don't put more logs on the fire. Don't look for more reasons to worry, criticize yourself, or feel mistreated. Don't get mad at yourself for getting mad at yourself!

When you throw second darts, you are the person you hurt most. The suffering—mild to severe—in second darts is truly unnecessary. As the saying goes, pain is inevitable, but suffering is optional.

46

Relax Anxiety about Imperfection

"Imperfections" are all around, and they include: messes, dirty clothes, weeds, snarled traffic, rain during a picnic, wine stains on carpet; injury, illness, disability, pain; problems, issues, obstructions, losses—including with others; objects that are chipped, frayed, broken; mistakes, errors; confusion, lack of clarity; war, famine, poverty, oppression, injustice.

In a nutshell, an imperfection—as I mean it here—is a departure from a reasonable ideal or standard (e.g., dog poop on your shoe is not ideal, nor is the hunger that afflicts one in six people worldwide). These departures-from-ideal have costs, and it's reasonable to do what you can about them.

But we usually don't leave it at that: we get *anxious*—uneasy, nervous, troubled, stressed—about imperfection itself, rather than recognizing it as a normal, unavoidable, and widespread aspect of life. Instead of dealing with conditions as they are—weeds, injuries, conflicts with others—and just handling them, we get caught up in worrying about what they mean, grumbling, feeling deflated, becoming opinionated and judgmental, blaming ourselves and others, and feeling woe-is-me and yet again disappointed/mistreated/wronged.

These reactions to imperfection are major second darts (as described in the previous chapter). They make you feel a lot worse than you need to, create issues with others, and make it harder to take skillful action.

Here's the alternative: let the broken cup be a broken cup without adding judgment, resistance, blaming, or worry to it.

How

Make appropriate efforts to improve things, but realize the impossibility of perfecting anything; even the most sophisticated technology cannot produce a *perfectly* flat table. You just can't perfect your personality, thoughts, or behavior; trying to do so is like trying to polish Jell-O. Nor can you perfect others or the world. Open to this fact: you cannot perfectly protect your loved ones, or eliminate all of your own health risks, or prevent people from doing stupid things. At first this opening could feel poignant or sad, but then you'll likely feel a breath of fresh air, a freedom, and a surge of energy to do the things you *can* now that you're not undermined by the hopelessness of making anything perfect.

We need standards and ideals—from the strike zone in baseball to the aspirations in the world's sacred teachings—but we also need to hold these lightly. Otherwise, they'll take on a life of their own in your mind, like petty tyrants barking orders: "You *must* do this, it's *bad* to do that." Watch out for righteousness, for self-important moralizing insistence on your own view of how you, others, and the world should operate. Know if you have tendencies toward perfectionism; I do, and I've got to be careful about them or I become a difficult person to live with or work for, as well as unhappy inside.

Further, many things transcend fixed standards. For example, could there ever be such a thing as a perfect rose or a perfect child? In these cases, anxiety about imperfection is absurd—which applies to trying to perfect your body, career, relationships, family, business, or spiritual practice. Nurture these, help them blossom, but give up on perfecting them.

Most fundamentally, all conditions, no matter how imperfect, are perfectly what they are: the bed is perfectly unmade, the milk is perfectly spilt. I don't mean morally or pragmatically "perfect"—as if it would be just perfect to tear a shirt or start a war—but that all conditions are utterly, thoroughly themselves. In this sense, whatever is the case—from dirty diapers and everyday hassles to cancer and plane crashes—is the result in this instant of the perfect unfolding of the entire universe. Try to see that unfolding as a vast, objective process in which our personal wishes are as consequential for it as a patch of foam is for the Pacific Ocean. In this light, perfection and imperfection vanish as meaningful distinctions. There are only things in their own right, in and of themselves, without our labels of good or bad, beautiful or ugly, perfect or not. Then there is no anxiety about imperfection; there is only simplicity, directness, engagement—and peace.

47

Respond, Don't React

To simplify the explanation of a complex journey, your brain evolved in three stages:

- ✦ Reptile, fish—Brainstem, focused on *avoiding* harm

- ✦ Mammal, bird—Limbic system, focused on *approaching* rewards

- ✦ Human—Cortex, focused on *attaching* to "us"

Whether a person is a psychopathic criminal or a saint, these three systems—avoiding, approaching, attaching— are always at work. The key is whether they're at work in a good way—one that promotes happiness and benefit for yourself and others—or a bad one that leads to suffering and harm.

What's happening in your brain when these systems are functioning in a good way—when you're feeling fine, or even "in the zone," self-actualizing, or spiritually blossoming? The answer is important, because then you can deliberately stimulate and thus gradually strengthen the neural networks that underpin these good states of mind.

When you are not rattled by life—in other words, when you're feeling safe, fulfilled, and loved—your brain's avoiding system is *calm* (in a word), the approaching system is *contented*, and the attaching system is *caring*. This is the *responsive* mode of the brain, which delights, soothes, and refuels you. It's your home base, the resting state of your brain, which is real good news.

Now here's the bad news: we also evolved hair-trigger mechanisms that activate the fight-or-flight *reactive* mode of the brain and drive us from home when we're stressed, whether from the snarl of a leopard a million years ago or a frown across a dinner table today. When you feel even subtly threatened, the avoiding system shifts gears into *hatred* (to use a strong, traditional word that encompasses the full range of fear and anger); when you're at all frustrated or dissatisfied, the approaching system tips into *greed* (ranging from longing to intense obsession or addiction); and when you feel even mildly rejected or devalued, the attaching system moves into *heartache* (from soft hurt to awful feelings of abandonment, worthlessness, or loneliness).

The reactive mode was a great way to keep our ancestors alive in the wild, and it's useful today in urgent situations. But it's lousy for long-term health and happiness. Each time your brain lights up its reactive mode—each time you feel pressured, worried, irritated, disappointed, let down, left out, or blue—this triggers the same stress machinery that evolved to escape charging lions or lethal aggression from other primates or humans.

Most reactive mode activations—pushing you off home base—are mild to moderate. But they're frequent and relentless in the lives of most people, leading to a kind of inner homelessness that can become the new normal. Besides feeling crummy, this is bad for your physical health, since chronic stress leads to a weakened immune system, disturbed digestion, dysregulated hormones, and increased risk of heart attack or stroke. Stress wears on your mental health as well, bringing: pessimism, blue mood, and depression; heightened anxiety and irritability; "learned helplessness"; hunkering down, playing it safe, dreaming smaller dreams; clutching tighter to "us" and fearing and even exploiting or attacking "them."

So—let's come home.

How

This book is full of practices for calm, contentment, and caring—and there are lots of other good methods in *Buddha's Brain* and in the writings and teachings of many people. So I'm not going to focus here on any particular way to activate the responsive mode of your brain. The key point is to make it a *priority* to feel good, to look for everyday opportunities for peacefulness, happiness, and love, and to take all the little moments you can to marinate in well-being.

Because here's more good news: Each time you rest in your brain's responsive mode, it gets easier to come home to it again. That's because "neurons that fire together, wire together": stimulating the neural substrates of calm, contentment, and caring *strengthens* them. This also makes it harder to be driven from home; it's like lengthening the keel of your mental sailboat so that no matter how hard the winds of life blow, you stay upright, not capsized, and keep on heading toward the lighthouse of your dreams.

What's wonderful about this is that the *ends* of the journey of life—being peaceful, happy, and loved/loving—become the *means* of getting there. In effect—in a traditional phrase—you are taking the fruit as the path. Instead of having to scratch and claw your way up the mountain top, you come home to the meadow that is the natural state of your brain—nourishing, expanding, and beautifying it every minute you spend there. For as they say in Tibet, "if you take care of the minutes, the years will take care of themselves."

48
Don't Take It Personally

Here's an updated parable from the ancient Taoist teacher Chuang-Tzu: Imagine that you are floating in a canoe on a slow-moving river, having a Sunday picnic with a friend. Suddenly there is a loud thump on the side of the canoe, and it rolls over. You come up sputtering, and what do you see? Somebody has snuck up on your canoe, flipped it over for a joke, and is laughing at you. How do you feel?

Okay. Now imagine the exact same situation again: the picnic in a canoe, loud thump, dumped into the river, coming up sputtering, and what do you see? A large submerged log has drifted downstream and bumped into your canoe. This time, how do you feel?

The facts are the same in each case: cold and wet, picnic ruined. But when you think you've been targeted *personally*, you probably feel worse. The thing is, most of what bumps into us in life—including emotional reactions from others, traffic jams, illness, or mistreatment at work—is like an impersonal log put in motion by ten thousand causes upstream.

Say a friend is surprisingly critical toward you. It hurts, for sure, and you'll want to address the situation, from talking about it with the friend to disengaging from the relationship.

But also consider what may have caused that person to bump into you, such as misinterpretations of your actions; health problems, pain, worries or anger about things unrelated to you; temperament, personality, childhood experiences; the effects of culture, economy, or world events; and causes back upstream in time, like how his or her parents were raised.

Recognize the humbling yet wonderful truth: most of the time, we are bit players in other people's dramas.

When you look at things this way, you naturally get calmer, put situations in context, and don't get so caught up in me-myself-and-I. Then you feel better, plus more clearheaded about what to do.

How

To begin with, have compassion for yourself. Getting smacked by a log is a drag. Also take appropriate action. Keep an eye out for logs heading your way, try to reduce their impact, and repair your "boat"—relationship, health, finances, career—as best you can. And maybe think about finding a new river!

Additionally:

* Notice when you start to take something personally. Be mindful of what that feels like—and also what it feels like to relax the sense of being personally targeted.

* Be careful about making assumptions about the intentions of others. Maybe they didn't do it "on purpose." Or maybe there was one not-so-good purpose aimed at you that was mixed up with a dozen other purposes.

* Reflect on some of the ten thousand causes upstream. Ask yourself: What else could be in play here? What's going on inside the other person's mind and life? What's the bigger picture?

* Beware getting caught up in your "case" about other people, driven by an inner prosecutor that keeps pounding on all the ways they're wrong, spoke badly, acted unfairly, picked on you, really really harmed you, made you suffer, etc., etc. It's good to see others clearly, and there's a place for moral judgment—but case-making is a kind of obsessing that makes you feel worse and more likely to overreact and create an even bigger problem.

* Try to have compassion for the other people. They're probably not all that happy, either. Your

compassion for them will not weaken you or let them off the moral hook; actually, it will make you feel better.

꙳ If you like, explore relaxing the sense of self—of *I* and *me* and *mine*—in general. For example, notice the difference between "there are sounds" and "I am hearing," or between "there are thoughts" and "I am thinking." Observe how the sense of self ebbs and flows, typically increasing when there are problems to solve and decreasing as you experience calm and well-being. This fluidity of "me" in the mind correlates with dynamic and fleeting activations in the brain; self-related thoughts are constructed all over the brain, tumbling and jostling with other thoughts, unrelated to self, in the neural substrates of the stream of consciousness (Gilliham and Farah 2005; Legrand and Ruby 2009). Appreciate that "I" is more of a process than an ability: a "selfing." Enjoy the ease and openness that emerge as the sense of self recedes.

And—really soak up the sense of strength and peacefulness that comes from taking life less personally.

49
Feel Safer

Consider these two mistakes:

1. You think there's a tiger in the bushes, but actually there isn't one.

2. You think there's no tiger in the bushes, but actually one is about to pounce.

Most of us make the first mistake much more often than the second one, for several reasons:

- Evolution has given us an anxious brain. In order to survive and pass on genes, it's better to make the first mistake a thousand times rather than make the second mistake even once; the cost of the first mistake is fear for no reason, but the cost of the second mistake could be death.

- This general tendency in the human brain is exacerbated by temperament—some people are naturally more anxious than others—and by life experiences (e.g., growing up in a dangerous neighborhood, experiencing trauma).

- Saturated with media, news about murders, disasters, economic turmoil, and horrible things happening to other people sifts into your mind—even though your own local situation is probably much less dangerous.

- In ways that have been repeated throughout history, political groups try to gain or hold onto power by exaggerating apparent threats.

In effect, most of us have a kind of paper tiger paranoia.

Certainly, it's important to recognize the real tigers in life, which come in many shapes and sizes: perhaps an impending layoff at work, a cough that won't go away, a teenager growing pot in the attic, a friend or coworker who keeps letting you down, or the health risks of smoking cigarettes. Try to notice any tendencies to overlook or minimize tigers, and do what you can about the ones that are real.

Meanwhile, try to recognize the ways that you—like most people—routinely overestimate threats while underestimating the resources inside you and around you. In effect, *most of us feel much less safe than we actually are.* The unfortunate results include unpleasant feelings of worry and anxiety; not hunkering down and reaching as high and wide as one might; stress-related illnesses; less capacity to be patient or generous with others; and a greater tendency to be snappish or angry (the engine of most aggression is fear). It's not good to feel like it's always Threat Level Orange!

Instead, feel as safe as you reasonably can.

How?

Some people get understandably nervous about feeling safer—since that's when you lower your guard, and things can really smack you. If this applies to you, adapt the suggestions here to your own needs, go at your own pace, and perhaps talk with a friend or counselor.

Further, there is no perfect safety in this life. Each of us will face disease, old age, and death, as well as lesser but still painful experiences. And many of us must deal with unsafe conditions in the community, workplace, or home.

This said, consider in your heart of hearts whether you deserve to feel safer: whether you are more braced against life, more guarded, more cautious, more anxious, more frozen, more appeasing, more rigid, or more prickly than you truly need to be.

If the answer is yes, here are some ways to help yourself feel safer, so that a growing internal sense of calm and confidence will increasingly match the true reality of the people and settings around you:

- Bring to mind the sense of being with someone who cares about you.

- Recall a time you felt strong.

- Recognize that you are in a protected setting.

- Mentally list some of the resources inside and around you that you could draw on to deal with what life throws you.

- Take a few breaths with l-o-n-g exhalations, and relax.

- All the while, keep helping yourself feel more sheltered, more supported, more capable, and safer. And less vigilant, tense, or fearful.

- Become more aware of what it's like to feel safer, and let those good feelings sink in, so you can remember them in your body and find your way back to them in the future.

You can practice with the methods above in general ways, such as in the morning plus several times a day if you tend to be fearful. Also try them in specific, unsettling situations, like before speaking up in a meeting, driving in traffic, getting on an airplane, or working through a sticky issue with your partner. Being on your own side, *help* yourself feel at least a little safer, and maybe a lot. Then see what happens. And take it in, again and again, if in fact, as they usually do, things turn out all right.

And there is really no tiger in the bushes after all.

50

Fill the Hole in Your Heart

As we grow up and then move through adulthood, we all have normal needs for safety, fulfillment, and love. For example, children need to feel secure, adolescents need a growing sense of autonomy, and young adults need to feel attractive and worthy of romantic love. When these needs are met by various "supplies"—such as the caring of a parent, the trust of a teacher, the love of a mate—the positive experiences that result then sink in to implicit memory to become resources for well-being, self-regulation, resilience, self-worth, and skillful action. This is how healthy psychological development is supposed to work.

But it doesn't always go this way, does it? In the lives of most people (me included)—even without any kind of significant mistreatment, trauma, or abuse—the incoming stream of supplies has sometimes been a thin soup: perhaps your parents were busy caring for a sick sibling or preoccupied with their own needs and conflicts, or you moved a lot as a kid and had a hard time connecting with peers, or high school was more than the usual social nightmare, or potential lovers were uninterested, or jobs have been frustrating and dispiriting, or . . . in other words, a typical life.

The shortages in a thin soup leave *lacks*, deficits, in key internal resources. For example, I was a year or two younger than my classmates, which led to a shortage of inclusion and valuing from them, which in turn led to a lack of confidence and sense of worth in groups that persisted into adulthood. The absence of good things naturally has consequences.

And so does the presence of bad ones. When blows land—when there is loss, mistreatment, rejection, abandonment, misfortune, or trauma—they leave *wounds*. Sometimes these heal fully, usually due to a rich soup of supplies. But often they don't, leaving pockets of unresolved emotional pain like pus beneath a scab, while also affecting a person's functioning like a lifelong limp from a broken ankle that never fully mended.

A lack or a wound will leave "a hole in your heart"—which gets even deeper when the two exacerbate each other. For example, I vividly recall the time a popular girl in high school really put me down; it was a minor blow in its own right, but my years of social isolation had left me with no shields or shock absorbers to buffer its impact, which was to make me feel awful about myself for a long time afterward.

So what can you do about your own lacks and wounds? You've got them; we all do. Life alone can be healing: time passes, you put more distance each year between yourself and the train wreck of your early childhood, seventh grade, first great love, last job, last marriage, or whatever, and you move on to a better place. But this essentially passive process of being carried by life is often not enough for a real healing: it's too slow, or it doesn't reach down deep enough, or key ingredients are missing.

Then you need to *actively* fill the hole in your heart.

How

It's fundamentally simple: you *take in good experiences* (chapter 2) that are specifically aimed at your own lacks and wounds. It's like being a sailor with scurvy: you need vitamin C—not vitamin E—for what ails you. For example, I felt both protected and independent as a child, so experiences of safety and autonomy as an adult—while valuable in their own right—did not address my issue: I needed the particular healing balm of experiences of inclusion and respect in groups.

Consequently, it's important to know what your own vitamin C is (and sometimes a person needs more than one kind). Perhaps you already know, but if not, here are some questions to help you find out: When your lacks or wounds developed, what would have made all the difference in the world? What do you long for today? What conditions help you feel truly happy—and bring out the best in you? What sort of experiences feed and soothe a deep hunger inside?

More specifically, here's a summary of some healing experiences—"vitamins"—targeted for particular lacks and wounds, organized in terms of the three motivational systems in your brain:

	Lack or Wound	**Vitamin**
Avoiding Harms	Weakness, helplessness	Strength, efficacy
	Alarm, anxiety	Safety, security
	Resentment, anger	Compassion for oneself and others
Approaching Rewards	Frustration, disappointment	Satisfaction, fulfillment
	Sadness, discontentment, "blues"	Gladness, gratitude
Attaching to "Us"	Not seen, rejected, left out	Attunement, inclusion
	Inadequacy, shame	Recognition, acknowledgement
	Abandonment, feeling unloved	Friendship, love

Once you have some clarity about the psychological vitamins you need, the rest is straightforward:

- Look for these vitamins in your life; also do what you can to create or increase them. For example, I keep my eyes open for opportunities to feel liked and appreciated in groups, plus I prod myself to join groups to create those opportunities.

- The vitamin you need is an *experience*, not an event. The point of situations in which you are protected, successful, or appreciated is to *feel* safe, fulfilled, and worthy. This is hopeful, because it gives you many ways to evoke key experiences. For example, if feeling that you matter to others is what will fill the hole in your heart, you could: look for signs that others wish you well, whether it's the smile of someone making you a sandwich in a deli, the encouragement of a coworker, or a lover's hug; think about the many people in your life today or in your past who like and appreciate you; ask your partner to be affectionate (and be open to hearing what would help him or her to do this); try to develop more relationships with people who are by nature warm and supportive.

- Be willing to get a slice of the pie if the alternative is no pie at all. For instance, if you finish a tough project at work, focus on the sense of accomplishment for everything you got done rather than on a few loose ends; if a friend is warm and loyal, open to feeling cared about even if what you really want is romantic love.

- Then, using the second and third steps of *taking in the good* (chapter 2), really savor the positive experience for ten or more seconds in a row while sensing that it is sinking down into you, giving you what you've always needed.

- Have confidence that every time you do this, you'll be wiring resources into your brain. When I started this practice myself, in my early twenties, the hole in my heart looked like the construction site for a skyscraper. But I just kept tossing a few bricks—a few experiences of feeling included—into that hole every day. One brick alone will make little difference, but brick after brick, day after day, year after year, you really can fill even a *very* big hole in your heart!

51
Let Go

I've done a lot of rock climbing, so I know firsthand the importance sometimes of *not* letting go! This applies to other things as well: keeping hold of a child's hand while crossing the street, staying true to your ethics in a tricky situation, or sustaining attention to your breath while meditating.

On the other hand, think of all the stuff—both physical and nonphysical—we cling to that creates problems for us and others: clutter in the home, "shoulds," rigid opinions, resentments, regrets, status, guilt, resistance to the facts on the ground, needing to be one-up with others, the past, people who are gone, bad habits, hopeless guests, unrewarding relationships, and so on.

Letting go can mean several things: releasing pain; dropping thoughts, words, and deeds that cause suffering and harm; yielding rather than breaking; surrendering to the way it is, like it or not; allowing each moment to pass away without trying to hold on to it; accepting the permanently impermanent nature of existence; and relaxing the sense of self and opening out into the wider world.

Living in this way is relaxing, decreases hassles and conflicts, reduces stress, improves mood and well-being, and grounds you in reality as it is. And it's a key element, if you like, of spiritual practice. To quote Ajahn Chah, a major Buddhist teacher who lived in Thailand:

If you let go a little, you will have a little happiness.

If you let go a lot, you will have a lot of happiness.

If you let go completely, you will be completely happy.

How

Appreciate the wisdom of letting go, and notice any resistance to it: perhaps it seems weak to you, foolish, or against the culture of your gender or personal background. For example, I remember talking with my friend John years ago about a woman he'd been pursuing who'd made it clear she wasn't interested, and he felt frustrated and hurt. I said maybe he should surrender and move on—to which John replied fiercely, "I don't *do* surrender." It took him a while to get past his belief that surrender—acceptance, letting go—meant you were wimping out. (All ended happily with us getting drunk together and him throwing up on my shoe—which *I* then had to surrender to!) It takes strength to let go, and fortitude, character, and insight. When you let go, you're like a supple and resilient willow tree that bends before the storm, still here in the morning—rather than a stiff oak that ends up broken and toppled over.

Be aware of the letting go that happens naturally all day long such as, releasing objects from your hands, hanging up the phone, pushing send on an e-mail, moving from one thought or feeling to another in your mind, saying bye to a friend, shifting plans, using the bathroom, changing a TV channel, or emptying the trash. Notice that letting go is all right, that you keep on going, that it's necessary and beneficial. Become more comfortable with letting go.

Consciously let go of tension in your body. Exhale long and slowly, activating the relaxing parasympathetic nervous system. Let go of holding in your belly, shoulders, jaws, and eyes.

Clear out possessions you don't use or need. Let in how great it feels to finally have some room in your closet, drawers, or garage.

Pick a dumb idea you've held on to way too long—one for me would be that I have to do things perfectly or there'll be a disaster. Practice dropping this idea and replacing it with better ones (like for me: "Nobody is perfect and that's okay").

Pick a grievance, grudge, or resentment—and resolve to move on. This does not necessarily mean letting other people off the moral hook, just that you are letting yourself off the hot plate of staying upset about whatever happened. If feelings such as hurt still come up about the issue, be aware of them, be kind to yourself about them, and then gently encourage them out the door.

Letting go of painful emotions is a big subject, with lots of resources for you in books such as *Focusing*, by Eugene Gendlin, or *What We May Be*, by Piero Ferrucci. Here's a summary of methods I like: relax your body; imagine that the feelings are flowing out of you like water; vent in a letter you'll never send, or out loud someplace appropriate; get things off your chest with a good friend; take in positive feelings to soothe and gradually replace the painful ones.

In general, let things be pleasant without grasping after them; let things be unpleasant without resisting them; let things be neutral without prodding them to get pleasant. Letting go undoes the craving and clinging that lead to suffering and harm.

Let go of who you used to be. Let yourself learn, grow, and therefore change.

Let go of each moment as it disappears beneath your feet. It's gone as soon as you're aware of it, like a snowflake melting as soon as you see its shape. You can afford to abide as letting go because of the miracle—which no scientist fully understands—that the next moment continually emerges as the previous one vanishes, all within the infinitely tiny duration of Now.

52
Love

We all want to *receive* love. But maybe it comes in a form you don't want—perhaps someone offers romantic love but that's not what you're looking for—or it doesn't come at all. Then there is heartache and helplessness; you can't make others love you if they won't.

Definitely, do what you can to get the love you need. But the practice here is about *expressing* love, distinct from receiving it. When you focus on the love you give rather than the love you get, then you're at cause rather than at effect; you're the cue ball, not the eight ball—which supports your sense of efficacy and confidence, as well as your mood. And it's enlightened self-interest: the best way to get love is to give it; even if it's still not returned, your love will likely improve the relationship, and help calm any troubled waters.

Sometimes people worry that being loving will make them vulnerable or drained. But actually, you can see in your own experience that love itself doesn't do this: it protects and nurtures you when you give it. While you're loving, don't you feel uplifted and stronger?

That's because love is deep in human nature, literally woven into our DNA. As our ancestors evolved, the seeds of love in primates and hominids—such as mother-child attachment, pair bonding, communication skills, and teamwork—aided survival, so the genes that promoted these characteristics were passed on. A positive cycle developed: As "the village it takes to raise a child" evolved and grew stronger, the period of vulnerable childhood could become longer, so the brain evolved to become larger in order to make use of that longer childhood—and thereby developed more capacities for love. The brain has roughly tripled in size since hominids began making stone tools about 2.5 million years ago, and much of this new neural real estate is devoted to love and related capabilities.

We need to give love to be healthy and whole. If you bottle up your love, you bottle up your whole being. Love is like water: it needs to flow; otherwise, it backs up on itself and gets stagnant and smelly. Look at the faces of some people who are very loving: they're beautiful, aren't they? Being loving heals old wounds inside and opens untapped reservoirs of energy and talent. It's also a profound path of awakening, playing a central role in all of the world's major religious traditions.

The world *needs* your love. Those you live with and work with need it, plus your family and friends, people near and far, and this whole battered planet. Never

underestimate the ripples spreading out from just one loving word, thought, or deed!

How

Love is as natural as breathing, yet like the breath, it can
get constricted. Sometimes you may need to release it,
strengthen it, and help it flow more freely with methods
like these:

- Bring to mind the sense of being with people
  who care about you, and then open to *feeling*
  cared about. Let this feeling fill you, warming
  your heart, softening your face. Sink into this
  experience. It's okay if opposite thoughts arise
  (e.g., rejection); observe them for a moment, and
  then return to feeling cared about—which will
  warm up the neural circuits of being loving
  yourself.

- Sense into the area around your heart, and think
  of things that evoke heartfelt feelings, such as
  gratitude, compassion, or kindness. To bring
  harmony to the tiny changes in the interval
  between heartbeats, breathe so that your inhala-
  tions and exhalations are about the same length,
  since inhaling speeds up the heart rate and
  exhaling slows it down. The heart has more than
  a metaphorical link to love; the cardiovascular
  and nervous systems lace together in your body

like lovers' fingers, and practices like these will nurture wholehearted well-being in you and greater warmth for others.

❧ Strengthen these loving feelings with soft thoughts toward others, such as *I wish you well. May you not be in pain. May you be at peace. May you live with ease.* If you feel upset with someone, you can include these reactions in your awareness while also extending loving thoughts like *I'm angry with you and won't let you hurt me again—and I still hope you find true happiness, and I still wish you well.*

There is a notion that being intentional about love makes it false or at least second-rate. But actually, loving at will is doubly loving: the love you find is authentic, and the effort to call it forth is deeply caring.

To love is to have *courage*, whose root meaning comes from the word "heart." I've been in a lot of hairy situations in the mountains, yet I was a lot more scared just before I told my first real girlfriend that I loved her. It takes courage to give love that may not be returned, to love while knowing you'll inevitably be separated one day from everything you love, to go all in with love and hold nothing back.

Sometimes I ask myself, *Am I brave enough to love?* Each day gives me, and gives you, many chances to love.

If you choose just one thing from this book of practices, let it be love.

References

Baumeister, R., E. Bratlavsky, C. Finkenauer, and K. Vohs. 2001. Bad is stronger than good. *Review of General Psychology* 5:323-370.

Berridge, K. C. and T. E. Robinson. 1998. What is the role of dopamine in reward: hedonic impact, reward learning, or incentive salience? Brain Research Reviews 28:309-369.

Davidson, R. J. 2004. Well-being and affective style: Neural substrates and biobehavioural correlates. *Philosophical Transactions of the Royal Society* 359:1395–1411.

Dusek, J. A., H. H. Out, A. L. Wohlhueter, M. Bhasin, L. F. Zerbini, M. G. Joseph, H. Benson, and T. A. Libermann. 2008. Genomic counter-stress changes induced by the relaxation response. *PLoS ONE* 3:e2576.

Farb, N. A. S., Z. V. Segal, H. Mayberg, J. Bean, D. McKeon, Z. Fatima, and A. Anderson. 2007. Attending to the present: Mindfulness meditation reveals distinct neural modes of self-reference. *Social Cognitive and Affective Neuroscience* 2:313–322.

Gillihan, S. J. and M. J. Farah. 2005. Is self special? A critical review of evidence from experimental psychology and cognitive neuroscience. *Psychological Bulletin*, 131:76-97.

Goetz, J. L., D. Keltner, and E. Simon-Thomas. 2010. Compassion: An evolutionary analysis and empirical review. *Psychological Bulletin* 136:351-374.

Gottman, J. 1995. *Why Marriages Succeed or Fail: And How You Can Make Yours Last*. New York: Simon and Schuster.

Gu, Y., J. W. Nieves, Y. Stern, J. A. Luchsinger, and N. Scarmeas. 2010. Food combination and Alzheimer disease risk: A protective diet. *Archives of Neurology* 67:699-706.

Guerrero-Beltran, C. E., M. Calderon-Oliver, J. Pedraza-Chaverri, and Y. I. Chirino. 2010. Protective effect of sulforaphane against oxidative stress: Recent advances. *Experimental and Toxicologic Pathology*. December 1. Epub ahead of print.

James, W. 1890. *The Principles of Psychology* (vol. 1). New York: Henry Holt.

Kabat-Zinn, J. 2003. Mindfulness-Based Interventions in Context: Past, Present, and Future. *Clinical Psychology: Science and Practice* 10: 144-156.

Kabat-Zinn, J., Lipworth, L., and Burney, R. 1985. The clinical use of mindfulness meditation for the self-regulation of chronic pain. *Journal of Behavioral Medicine* 8:163-190.

Krikorian, R., M. D. Shidler, T. A. Nash, W. Kalt, M. R. Vinqvist-Tymchuk, B. Shukitt-Hale, and J. A. Joseph. 2010. Blueberry supplementation improves memory in older adults. *Journal of Agriculture and Food Chemistry* 58:3996-4000.

Kristal-Boneh, E., M. Raifel, P. Froom, and J. Ribak. 1995. Heart rate variability in health and disease. *Scandinavian Journal of Work, Environment, and Health* 21:85–95.

Lazar, S., C. Kerr, R. Wasserman, J. Gray, D. Greve, M. Treadway, M. McGarvey, B. Quinn, J. Dusek, H. Benson, S. Rauch, C.

Moore, and B. Fischl. 2005. Meditation experience is associated with increased cortical thickness. *NeuroReport* 16:1893–1897.

Leary, M., E. Tate, C. Adams, A. Allen, and J. Hancock. 2007. Self-compassion and reactions to unpleasant self-relevant events: The implications of treating oneself kindly. *Journal of Personality* 92:887–904.

Legrand, D. and P. Ruby. 2009. What is self-specific? Theoretical investigation and critical review of neuroimaging results. *Psychological Review* 116:252-282.

Maguire, E., D. Gadian, I. Johnsrude, C. Good, J. Ashburner, R. Frackowiak, and C. Frith. 2000. Navigation-related structural change in the hippocampi of taxi drivers. *Proceedings of the National Academy of Sciences* 97:4398–4403.

Maier, S. F. and L. R. Watkins. 1998. Cytokines for psychologists: Implications of bidirectional immune-to-brain communication for understanding behavior, mood, and cognition. *Psychological Review* 105:83-107.

McCullough, M. E., S. D. Kilpatrick, R. A. Emmons, and D. B. Larson. 2001. Is gratitude a moral affect? *Psychological Bulletin* 127:249-266.

Neff, K. D. 2009. Self-Compassion. In M. R. Leary and R. H. Hoyle, eds., *Handbook of Individual Differences in Social Behavior* (pp. 561-573). New York: Guilford Press.

Niedenthal, P. 2007. Embodying emotion. *Science* 316:1002.

Nimitphong, H. and M. F. Holick. 2011. Vitamin D, neurocognitive functioning and immunocompetence. *Current Opinion in Clinical Nutrition and Metabolic Care* 14:7-14.

Pecina, S, K. S. Smith, and K. C. Berridge. 2006. Hedonic hot spots in the brain. *The Neuroscientist* 12:500-511.

Rondanelli, M., A. Giacosa, A. Opizzi, C. Pelucchi, C. La Vecchia, G. Montorfano, M. Negroni, B. Berra, P. Politi, and A. M.

Rizzo. 2010. Effect of omega-3 fatty acids supplementation on depressive symptoms and on health-related quality of life in the treatment of elderly women with depression: A double-blind, placebo-controlled, randomized clinical trial. *Journal of the American College of Nutrition* 29:55-64.

Rozin, P. and E. B. Royzman. 2001. Negativity bias, negativity dominance, and contagion. *Personality and Social Psychology Review* 5:296-320.

Schiepers, O. J. G., M. C. Wichers, and M. Maes. 2005. Cytokines and major depression. *Progress in Neuro-Pharmacology & Biological Psychiatry* 29:210-217.

Seligman, M. E. P. 1972. Learned helplessness. *Annual Review of Medicine* 23:407-412.

Skarupski, K. A., C. Tangney, H. Li, B. Ouyang, D. A. Evans, and M. C. Morris. 2010. Longitudinal association of vitamin B_6, folate, and vitamin B_{12} with depressive symptoms among older adults over time. *The American Journal of Clinical Nutrition* 92:330-335.

Stein, D. J., V. Ives-Deliperi, and K. G. F. Thomas. 2008. Psychobiology of mindfulness. *CNS Spectrum* 13:752-756.

 **Rick Hanson, PhD,** is a neuropsychologist and author of *Buddha's Brain*, which has been published in twenty languages. He is founder of the Wellspring Institute for Neuroscience and Contemplative Wisdom and an Affiliate of the Greater Good Science Center at the University of California, Berkeley. He has been invited to lecture at Oxford, Stanford, and Harvard, and teaches in meditation centers worldwide. He lives with his family in the greater San Francisco Bay Area. For many resources freely offered, visit www.rickhanson.net.

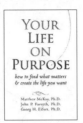